Cycling's World Championships: The Inside Story

Les Woodland

McGann Publishing
McMinnville, Oregon

Published by McGann Publishing
P.O. Box 864
McMinnville, OR 97128
USA

www.mcgannpublishing.com

McGann
Publishing

ISBN 978-0-9859636-7-5

Table of Contents

Introduction
The Rainbow Dream

If you've never tried on a yellow T-shirt and fancied yourself as leader of the Tour de France, it's because you have no soul or better dress sense. It's harder to copy the rainbow jersey of world champion, but the conceit of trying would be even greater. Apart from anything else, you get to wear a yellow jersey only on the day you're leading the Tour. The rainbow jersey, on the other hand, you wear all year and then, to show off, you wear rainbows on the cuffs of your racing shirts for the rest of your life.

I ask you: which is the better deal? Or a bigger fraud, because they're not the colors of a rainbow at all.

Cycling used to be like boxing: almost anyone who cared to could call his race a world championship. And under any rules. The British, for instance, held a world championship on a track in Leicester back in March, 1883. The bike industry put it on as a publicity drive, probably because the change had started towards newfangled bikes with chains or treadles and the industry wanted to get people to change. The promoters felt disgruntled when a Frenchman, Frédéric de Civry, swept past the rest on a penny-farthing.

There was already enough commercialism in the sport that riders were represented by agents who got them races. De Civry's was the English toff, Herbert Duncan, who lived in Paris and persuaded the owner of the Folies Bergère to put up the money for the city's first decent track. He took a commission of the fees paid anywhere he could place his riders. Having de Civry win in Leicester persuaded him to send the still better Charles Terront to the world's first six-day race, in Islington, London, and to another British promotion, a so-called 100-mile championship of the world. He won it, in 5 hours 58 minutes 20 seconds.

Les Woodland

The problem with this story is that you'd expect to find that championship in the list of prominent dates published by British Cycling, the modern-day national federation. But it's not there. It doesn't mention a world championship before Chicago in 1893, by which time the whole affair had been standardized.

To this day, there are world championships you perhaps never realized existed. There are championships for cycle-speedway, a sport dreamed up by kids who couldn't afford motorbikes but wanted to race round bomb sites. If you thought that BMX was the first time cycling copied motorcycling, you now know it wasn't. There are all the predictable championships—on the road, on the track, across fields. But there are championships for cycling prettily and even for delivering parcels and producing long skids. And I bet you didn't know that the most persistent world champions of all time, and entitled to wear the rainbow jersey, weren't road or track heroes but two Czechoslovakian brothers who cornered the sport of cycle-ball.

There has, of course, been plenty of treachery and trickery in world championships. The races are unusual in cycling in being contested, with the single exception of the team time trial on the road, by teams representing nations rather than sponsors. And even the team time trial was for national teams before 2012. The reason is that the governing body, the *Union Cycliste Internationale*, is just that: a union of national federations. It was born in Paris in 1900 during the Olympic Games and it's stuck to the Olympic principle that competitors compete individually but, if they have to be grouped at all, it's by nation.

The rest of the year, the world's best riders ride in teams paid for by the companies whose names are printed gaudily on their chest, back and, sadly, their backsides. Trade teams are built of riders from any number of countries. It is to those sponsors that they owe their primary allegiance. And that can bring problems. You may be American and I may be French and therefore we'll be in different national teams for the championship. But if you happen to be the boss of my everyday team—and the man who'll decide if I'll stay in a job for another year—I may be inclined not to beat you, and even to contrive for you to beat everyone else. Including other Frenchmen.

More complicated still, I may be from a smaller nation with no clear leader or even ambition. If I can't win myself, there's an attraction in accepting a pile of notes to ride for someone else instead: anybody who needs help and has the cash to pay for it.

At least the problem of amateurs and professionals is over. One of the concerns that led to the creation of the UCI in the first place was that the founders of the first world body—who happened to be the British—would accept only national federations that shared their own puritanical translation of "amateur". The word is French and, in French, it doesn't have the meaning it has in English. It means an enthusiast, someone who enjoys something but doesn't make a living from it. A profit, maybe, but not a living. That's not quite the same as the British demand that winners get nothing more than clocks, cups and cutlery.

The first big shamateurism came with the American sprinter, Arthur Zimmerman. He liked what he was doing to the extent that, for a single one-mile race at Springfield, Massachusetts, in 1892, he won a buggy and two horses to pull it, total value twice the average annual wage. In that one year, said the *New York Times*, he won "29 bicycles, several horses and carriages, half a dozen pianos, a house and a lot [of ground], household furniture of all descriptions, and enough silver plates, medals and jewelry to stock a jewelry store."

But no cash, so he stayed an amateur. Only the British objected, finally tripping him up on a trip to London when they worked out a link between him, his Raleigh bicycle, the Raleigh posters in which he appeared and the house which Raleigh had provided to accommodate him. They banned him. Sadly for them, nobody else cared and he went off to race elsewhere.

Earnings like that would be acceptable to full-scale professionals even now. But they are at least openly paid. Less obviously paid were riders from countries in the Soviet zone of the 1950s onwards. The communist creed refused professionalism in sport, while at the same time seeing it as war by another means. The idea that the best Soviet riders rarely had to work down a mine and then go training in the evening with a rear light swinging under their saddle wasn't often contested. And even in the west, governments found jobs for talented cyclists, as policemen or some other job with limited hours and unlimited leave. Raleigh, never slow to make the most of talented amateurs, gave a long-distance amateur of the 1950s a bike and employed him as a saddle-tester. And those who couldn't get that luck could get by on unemployment pay and prizes illegally received in cash.

The outcome: cycling and the Olympics gave up. There is now no distinction between amateur and professional, only between those younger or older than 23. Eastern countries abandoned their prissiness—it was that or not ride at all—and the end of the communist experiment turned some of the region's riders into the most capitalist of all.

This capitalism produced another effect: some professional teams would prefer their riders not to win championships. Because cycling has distinctive jerseys for national and world champions, and insists they wear them, the champions of whom a team ought to boast are less obviously part of the team because they're kitted out differently. The Festina team of the 1990s was not the first to discourage riders from winning championships; the sponsors didn't see it as commercially worthwhile.

There was a time, to the end of the 1960s, when the glamor and glory of a national or world champion's jersey was enough. It carried no advertising. Sometimes, the world champion didn't even wear a number. And then it changed. It's easy to say when. It was at the professional road race in 1965. Tom Simpson went to accept his gold medal not in the blue jersey with red sleeves he'd worn the rest of the day but in the white jersey circled by checkered band of Peugeot. And he rode for all the following year with his sponsor's name embroidered on his jersey, against the rules and the first time it had been done.

Why? Because his position in the team was threatened by a young Belgian called Eddy Merckx. Professional teams then could have only two or three foreign riders. If there was room for Merckx then Simpson could lose not only his team leadership but even his contract. So wearing his trade jersey was worth the fine because it was a reminder not of what he had done for Britain but what he had done for a brand of bicycles. And the UCI, once the proud defender of a champion's glory, gave up. Advertising on the rainbow jersey grew until it looked as commercial—or cheap—as all the other garish jerseys. National jerseys have become even less distinguishable. All the UCI asks now is that riders wait until next morning before covering the once-hallowed jersey with advertisements for floor tiles or insurance.

Cycling's World Championships

Does this matter? Yes, it does. It cheapens the glory. And when glory is cheap, it has no value. But we haven't reached that far yet. There are still world championships and there are still world champions and there are still some wonderful stories! Join me on a trip to the crock at the other end of the rainbow!

Chapter 1: 1892 – 1909
Finding the World's Greatest – Rough Beginnings

1892
The first world championships

One of the joys of a world in which it is difficult to travel is that national championships could be safely opened to whoever turned up. A couple of foreigners on the bill made for better ticket sales back when many people hadn't gone further than the edge of their town. That explains why Americans can be found in the records of European championships, particularly the troublesome Arthur Zimmerman.

Since cycling was mainly European in the 19th century, European races and, especially, those in Britain, had the highest status. English championships became de facto world championships. That was an advantage for the home country but it made the rest of the world less attractive. No race they could ride at home would have the status of what they could ride abroad.

The idea of changing this situation, of establishing cycling internationally, came from the National Cyclists Union in London, and specifically from Henry Sturmey of *The Cyclist* and later founder of Sturmey-Archer, the hub gear company. He was a doughty figure with a generous white beard and mustache and thin-framed glasses beneath eyebrows darker than his hair. He was a true heavyweight in 19th-century cycling, even if later he went off to direct the Daimler car company and edit *Autocar*.

Sturmey wanted standard rules and true world championships. And so the NCU wrote around the world to propose an International

Cycling Association. Most countries agreed quickly but Italy hesitated, because nobody could be found to speak English, and it didn't join until 1898.

The ICA began in Islington, London, in November 1892 and held its first world championships in Chicago the following year. They were part of the World's Fair and received little attention. Zimmerman won the sprint and 10 kilometers and Lawrence Meintjes of South Africa the motor-paced race.

There were then further championships in Antwerp (1894), Cologne (1895), Copenhagen (1896), Glasgow (1897), Vienna (1898) and Montreal (1899).

1895
A poke in the eye

Things didn't always go smoothly. It was in Cologne in 1895 that professionals were first allowed to ride. In all, something like 60 riders, amateur and professional, came from eleven countries. But many refused to go. Germany used the championships to flaunt its victory in the Franco-Prussian war 25 years earlier, which had ended with the siege of Paris, and the bad taste offended. French riders are noticeably absent from the medalists.

Robert Protin, a long-faced Belgian from Liège, was riding the professional sprint final against the round-faced American, Georgie Banker of Pittsburgh, and another Belgian, Émile Huet. Protin lined up closest to the starter who, as he started the race, poked the flag in Protin's eye. Protin, predictably, lost the race.

He then complained and the riders were told to race again. Banker refused. He'd won and he was world champion, he said. The judges told him he wasn't and that the ride was going to be run again regardless and that he'd better cooperate if he wanted to be the champion, something he thought he already was. So they rode again and this time Protin won.

Banker didn't give up. He complained that he had been demoralized, that he'd seen a shadow across the track and mistaken it for the finish line, and he whined enough that he started getting support. The International Cycling Association thought about it for weeks, then canceled both races and called for another final. Belgium, of course, took offense at that and said it would leave the ICA rather than see its man challenged. The ICA wasn't firmly enough established to lose one of its members and it backed down and Protin stayed world champion. It wasn't a bad choice: he was national champion in 1891, 1892, 1893 and 1894, national 100-kilometer champion in 1893, European sprint champion in 1892 and 1893, French open 5-kilometer champion in 1893, and the world 500-meter record holder in 1895.

Banker stayed in Europe and won the *grands prix* of Antwerp and Roubaix in 1894. He then contracted typhoid before recovering and winning in Austria, Tunisia and Belgium in 1898 and 1899. In 2010, the Heinz History Center began installing an area for cycling and for Banker.

The motor-paced event went to the Welshman, Jimmy Michael, a professional with Dunlop, only seven years after John Boyd Dunlop fitted pneumatic tires to a bicycle wheel. Michael was 18, little more than five feet tall, more like a doll than a teenager. He was the hero of European tracks, cheered wherever he went because of his apparent childlike vulnerability.

His manager was a shady-looking man called James "Choppy" Warburton, who dressed theatrically in long overcoats from which he'd produce mysterious bottles and run to hand them to his riders. Nobody knows whether he was respectable, a charlatan or the man who popularized drug-taking in cycling. Whatever he was, he was disreputable enough that the British warned him off, meaning he wasn't banned but that he wasn't welcome at tracks.

Warburton's other star, Arthur Linton, won Bordeaux–Paris in 1896, and died from typhus at 27. His brother Tom, another of Warburton's protégés, died also of typhus at 39. By 1899 Michael had spent all his money on drink and gambling—he was briefly a jockey and owned horses—and in 1903 he had to be pulled out of a bar close to the Arc de Triomphe at the moment a crowd was waiting to see him ride at the Buffalo velodrome on the city's edge. He died of alcohol poisoning on a liner taking him to America, where he hoped to restart his career and pay his debts. He was 27. His death was blamed on "fatigue fever". The truth of Warburton's involvement with Michael and the others will never be known, but he remains the common factor.

Les Woodland

1899
The ride of the Black Cyclone

Marshall Taylor, better known as "Major", rode the 1899 championship and became cycling's first black champion and only the second black world champion in any sport. The first was the Canadian boxer, George Dixon, in 1890. Taylor won the mile championship on the Queen's Park velodrome in Montreal, the first time he had been abroad.

The *Montreal Gazette* wrote: "Fast and furious, they came around the last turn. Within sight of the line, the colored rider crouched lower than ever over his mount and made a finish that would have caused the most sensational of them all to turn green with envy. Major Taylor fairly lifted himself and his wheel [his bicycle] across the line."

Taylor himself recalled: "I shall never forget the thunderous applause that greeted me. I thrilled as I heard the band strike up the *Star Spangled Banner*. My national anthem took on a new meaning for me from that moment."

Taylor was always more popular in Europe than in America, where he was born and where he was regularly rejected because of his color. He beat the one-mile national track record when he was 15 and was then "hooted" by the crowd because he was black. He never overcame that rejection in his home land and died a pauper after going door to door to sell his life story in the hope of a little money.

Many Europeans didn't go to the championships in Canada, because of the distance and because of the cycling politics in North America. Many of the USA's best professionals belonged to a rebel body, the American Racing Cyclists Union, and the union argued to the ICA that they should also take part. If they didn't, the championships wouldn't be worth their name, they insisted. But Henry Sturmey threw out the idea. His ICA recognized the League of American Wheelmen and there wasn't room for two national bodies from any country and so the union's riders had to stay home and sulk and hope for better times.

1900
Revolt and the first modern championships

Britain is not one country. It is a federation of nations and within the ICA it insisted on separate teams and administrators for England,

Cycling's World Championships

Scotland and Ireland and would have done for Wales if, for some reason, it hadn't been left out. It was an obvious situation for the British and one that still applies in the Commonwealth Games. But the French would have nothing of it and it objected that that gave Britain too many votes and too many riders.

George Stancer, a heavyweight of English cycling, remembered: "This domination was more apparent than real, for the NCU exercised no control or influence over the independent governing bodies of Scotland, Ireland, Australia, South Africa and Canada." Which was to miss the point that the French, and then others, were making: that there were just too many teams.

For a while, things went on as they were. But the grumbling continued. The NCU, when it invited other countries to join the ICA, had gone only to organizations that shared its strict definition of amateurism. Historian Jim McGurn said:

> The National Cyclists' Union [until 1883 the Bicycle Union], made itself unpopular in the early 1890s for its stubborn and seemingly nit-picking opposition to riders who professed themselves "amateur."

> The national organizations which governed cycle sport were often in dispute, largely as a result of their varying attitudes to the spread of professionalism. The Bicycle Union, having quarreled with the Amateur Athletics Association over cycle race jurisdiction on AAA premises, took issue with the *Union Vélocipèdique de France* over the French body's willingness to allow its "amateurs" to compete for prizes of up to 2,000 francs, the equivalent of about 16 months' pay for a French manual worker. The Bicycle Union often refused to recognize the amateur licenses of visiting UVF competitors, and eventually broke off relations on the grounds that the UVF allowed mixed amateur-professional events.

France became represented instead by the cycling branch of a large athletic club which, *Scottish Cyclist* said, "no more represents French cyclists than, say, the Edinburgh University CC does Scottish cyclists."

The 1900 world championships were planned for Paris. And, there, the French saw their chance. The countries taking part sent representatives to the usual pre-championship meeting. And there the British heard the French demand that "England" should send just one team, a team that would represent not just the British Isles but the whole of the Empire.

The meeting was adjourned and another date set. But in April the French said they were starting a new body, the Union Cycliste Internationale, and that "England" could join but only on French conditions. Stancer had no immediate reply. He couldn't act alone. He'd have to ask the NCU. But by that time the UCI had already been set up with the agreement of the Italy, Switzerland and the USA, which had appointed a Frenchman, Victor Breyer, the future deputy organizer of the Tour de France, to represent it, and a short time afterward Holland and Germany. Lobbying had being going on without Britain's knowing.

Britain was left to sail on in the *Marie Celeste* of the ICA. It sniffed and said it would organize its own world championships but little more was heard of them or the ICA.

The UCI therefore came into existence on April 14, 1900, further distancing itself from the British and their empire by abolishing the mile and setting the sprint at 2,000 meters. It has governed world cycling ever since, although there are still rebel federations around the world. Britain, which invented international cycling, had to spend a year in the cold before it could ask to join the club it had inspired and which had rejected it. It finally signed up in February, 1903, still for a while with votes for England Ireland, Scotland and Wales. Australia joined the following August.

The motivation to start the UCI and to base it in Paris came from the Olympic Games being held in the city. The Games were second of the series and the first outside Greece. Their founder, Pierre de Coubertin, proposed Paris because it was his home capital. Another 14 years were to pass before the Games adopted the five colored rings that are now its symbol but, all events added together, there was a powerful motivation for the UCI to use the same colors, although not the rings, on the jerseys it awarded to world champions.

The Olympic movement is jealous of its five rings and the UCI has its own variation as a trademark. Which hasn't stopped roller-skating using it.

Cycling's World Championships

1904
All-American hold-up

London in 1904 was a squalid place. The affluent corridors of Piccadilly and Mayfair glittered with jewelry and the carriages of the well-to-do. But only streets away, abject poverty was little better than it had been a century earlier. One in five children died in their first year. Pneumonia and TB were rampant.

Most Londoners that summer had no idea that Americans were sweeping up medals at the world cycling championships on the grounds of the glittering Crystal Palace in the countryside beyond southern London.

The American hold-up was complete: Bobby Walthour won the motor-paced championship, Iver Lawson the professional sprint and Marcus Hurley the amateur sprint. Lawson, says Peter Nye, was lucky to ride at all; he had been suspended for a year for causing a crash in front of 20,000 people in Melbourne, Australia, thereby putting his rival in hospital for two weeks. He appealed and had his ban cut to three months, which let him ride the world championship.

Of Walthour, Andrew Homan wrote: "1904 was the kind of career year that few professional athletes experience. Contrary to today's trend and the overwhelming attention given to the Tour de France, in 1904 road racing was not as popular as track racing, and no other rider in the world could sell out a track stadium like Walthour. For a few years he ruled as king of the cycling world, and a very dangerous world it was."

Walthour was often as horizontal as he was upright. *The Washington Post* marked his cycling retirement in 1915 by pointing out that he broke his collar bone 45 times, snapped 30 ribs and 6 fingers, had 40 stitches in his legs and 60 stitch marks in his face. Before adding: "He has been pronounced dead twice and fatally injured at least six times."

Some of that came from motor-paced riding. Paced riding had until then been behind quintets: bicycles with seating for five. Replacing them by powerful but primitive motorcycles increased both the speed and the danger, because there was little regulation and because the motorbike could so easily and disastrously blow up. Or, in the days before the rules insisted on a roller behind the rear fender to keep the rider at a distance, a touch of the front wheel could equally send a rider to his death.

Walthour's counterpart in the amateur race at Crystal Palace was a Londoner, Leon Meredith. He amply demonstrated the dangers of the game. He went straight into the lead and after 30 kilometers he had five laps on the rest. But then his motorbike broke down and decelerated, so that Meredith rode into the back of it at speed and rolled across the track, turning somersaults. He got back up, blood running, and won the race on another bike and with a different pacer. People were made differently then.

Meredith also rode well on the road. Bill Bailey, the Briton who won the world amateur sprint four times, said of Meredith: "He was one of the most versatile riders I ever saw, winning races from a quarter-mile to six hours. Usually when thinking of motor-paced riders, we regard them as specialists who, once they have adopted the little front wheel, reversed forks and big gears, are somehow never able to show good form in normal competition. Meredith was an exception. He mixed his racing most successfully and, in 1910, when he had already been world champion five times, astounded the cycling world by becoming the first rider ever to beat five hours for an unpaced out-and-home 100 [miles] on the road."

Meredith's cycling career ended, after seven world championship wins—in 1904, 1905, 1907, 1908, 1909, 1911 and 1913, when war began in 1914. He created the Constrictor cycling wholesale business, its products still fondly remembered by elderly British cyclists. He died at 47 while skiing in Switzerland.

1909
Bill Bailey comes home

The 1909 championships in Copenhagen marked the start of a quartet of gold medals by British sprinter Bill Bailey, the one who so praised Leon Meredith. He won the world sprint in 1901, 1910, 1911 and 1913 and, the next prestigious race, the Grand Prix de Paris, every year from 1910 to 1913. The war ended his amateur career, but as a professional he came third in the world championship of 1920, in Antwerp. In 1908 he set a British amateur record for the mile at 58 seconds, and 20 years later set the professional record at 57.6 seconds. He died in London in 1971, when he was 82.

Chapter 2: Early 1920s
Secret Championships?

1920
Big Bob Spears

He was built like a statue of old, wrote the French historian, Pierre Chany. And he came out of nowhere to snatch world sprinting from those who thought they had it in the bag. His name was Bob Spears, 1 meter 85 (6'1") tall, 85 kilograms (187 pounds) fresh out of the bath tub, "a man so handsome that you caught your breath." And with all the social grace you'd expect of a son of an Australian sheep farmer.

Nobody knew who he was when he turned up to train on the track at Vincennes, near Paris. But they soon learned. He had won a six-day race in Melbourne in 1913 and come second in another in Sydney. He went to America the same year, invited by Alf Goullet—whom the American organizer mogul John Chapman had told to find him two good Australians—and won the five-mile championship of Vailsburg.

In 1914 he won the American three-mile championship and in 1918 he won 27 races to become the American all-round champion. Yet all they knew of him when he went to Europe in 1919 was that he knew how to throw a boomerang, which he taught in the track center to anyone who cared.

That changed when he won the first of three Grand Prix de Paris in 1920. And then three weeks later he went north to Antwerp for the first world championship after the war. There he outsprinted Ernest Kaufmann of Switzerland and the Briton, Bill Bailey, by riding languidly to the last 100 meters and then coming down the track's slope to win by a length.

One historian said: "His method in racing was to take as little as possible out of himself to gain first place, to win with the least effort.

Spears would never try to win by a hundred yards when a few inches would do the trick."

He came second in 1921 and 1922 but by then his best had passed. He vanished as quickly as he'd appeared. His hometown of Dubbo named two streets after him, though. Later, the same town erased him from public history. Spears Drive and Spears Park were renamed in an effort to change the tone of the area, which the *Daily Liberal* said "was labeled one of the state's most notorious social housing precincts." A riot by 100 people after years of law and order problems ended with houses being destroyed and a police car set on fire.

1921
First amateur road championship

It seems obvious now that there should be a world championship on the road. But back then, road racing seemed too chancy, too hit and miss, too affected by tactics, compared to the purity of the sprint and pursuit. And what about the extra work and organization? How could a championship break even if spectators could stand beside the road for nothing? But the Italians liked the idea and began canvassing support for the next meeting of the UCI, in 1920. France liked the idea, too, which helped because the UCI would meet in Paris. The Swiss and Belgians joined in, and the British became interested when the meeting suggested not open road-racing but a time trial.

The first world road championship started in Glostrup, outside Copenhagen, in 1921, and set off on a circuit of 190 kilometers with a control at around half distance where riders would dismount to sign in. That seems odd now but it was the convention of early road racing, including the Tour de France, in which few marshals were appointed and riders were given a list of towns and places to sign a check list to show they'd not taken short cuts.

The continental idea of time trialing was far removed from the religious purity of what the British had established. That had been obvious in the Olympics around Lake Malar in Sweden in 1912, when great groups formed on the road and fought out a time trial as though it were a road race. The British hoped that lessons had been learned. But the British hoped in vain.

Cycling's World Championships

Britain's Charlie Davey passed a Frenchman who then sat behind him until they caught another Frenchman. The French then combined to drop Davey, who couldn't keep up on an 83-inch fixed wheel. The extra speed of trying to keep up must have helped, though, because he finished third, 35 seconds behind Willum Nielsen of Denmark but almost 5 minutes behind the winner, the rugged, square-jawed Gunnar Sköld of Sweden.

Sköld went on to ride the Olympics, where he won a team medal in the road race. Charlie Davey, a lifelong vegetarian with a long face and a blunt chin who'd come into cycling only after trying soccer and running, finished in the first three the next year as well, when Britain ran the championships in a cloud of secrecy. He turned professional in 1936, set distance records and rode the Bol d'Or track race in Paris. He raced until he was 40 and judged and kept time at races into his 70s. He died aged 78 in October, 1964.

1921
Pieter the Great

The Copenhagen championships were the first of five triumphs in the sprint for the lanky Dutch sprinter, Piet Moeskops. He beat the equally tall Bob Spears in Copenhagen and then again the following year in Paris. He won the world sprint every year from 1921 to 1924 and then again in 1926.

A row broke out in Holland after one championship win, when Moeskops took a Dutch flag he'd been given and held it to his handlebars as he took a lap of honor. For days afterward the letters columns of newspapers complained that he hadn't treated the flag with respect.

1922
The secret championships

Have you ever heard of the world championship that nobody was allowed to know about? No? Well, it was held in Britain in 1922. And it fell afoul of a British worry that racing on the road might be illegal. A woman riding a horse and buggy had been startled by "road scorchers" at the end of the nineteenth century and the British, scared that the police and then the government would ban all cycling on the road if they carried on, told clubs to promote races only on the track in future.

Not everybody lived near a track, though, and so a rebel body organized races at dawn and in such secrecy that the courses and dates were kept secret even in the cycling press and riders wore black from neck to ankle to somehow make them less obvious. And riders would start at intervals and race not between themselves but against the clock, so that if the police found out the promoters could insist it wasn't a race.

No police force in the world would be so stupid as not to realize what was happening but this pretense of secrecy was still in place in 1922. In fact it continued for more than 40 years after that. The world championship road race was therefore held as a time trial, on a course through Shropshire in western England kept secret to the world, and in which the British riders wore black. This, of course, riders from more enlightened and more colorful countries found comical.

They were less amused when three of the black hangmen, Dave Marsh, Charles Burkhill and Charlie Davey, took the first three places and the team prize. Riding 100 miles alone has to be learned, but the British knew nothing else. Little Dave Marsh won by 1 minute 20 seconds. But not without controversy. *Cycling* said British riders had shouted for "stimulants." *Rad Welt* of Germany went further: "The English amateurs were full of [drugs] and all the other amateurs showed every indication that they also had taken dope."

The NCU knew the only way it could run a road race was as a time trial. But it had banned time trialling in 1888 and prohibited "any of its officials from officiating or assisting at any road races." And it gave the job of organization to the Anfield Bicycle Club in Liverpool, which only a year earlier had been organizing rebel time trials and cocking its fingers at the NCU.

The Anfield Club chose the track at New Brighton, across the Mersey from Liverpool. It was in an athletics and cycling stadium behind the Tower building. It was almost flat and 586 yards round, big enough that motorbike racing had been held there when motorbikes weren't too fast. The British thought it excellent but, by world standards, it was awful. The cement-and-gravel surface was good when it was laid in 1898 but by 1922 the weather had joined in and the world had moved on and the motor-paced events were taken away before the championships even began.

The track was also treacherous if it got damp, and Liverpool is one of the wettest cities in England. The Dutchman, Piet Moeskops, "attempted a trial spin but his machine slipped on the greasy surface and he returned limping slightly and shaking his head," wrote the *Wallasey and Wirral Chronicle*. A new stand for 40,000 never housed more than 8,000 because the British knew little of track racing unless they happened to have lived near a track. The cycling press was largely about time trialling and utilitarian problems such as foxing…the police. The promoters had to appeal in local papers for businesses to advertise in the program.

The UCI then took away everything else. All the outstanding events were held in Paris. When the organizers began refunding tickets, spectators joined queues for more expensive tickets than they held. Money was handed back without question, given the fiasco.

1922
While waiting for a real championship

Every country found itself a champion, but who was the champion of champions? That's what the GP Wolber set out to find between 1922 and 1931. It brought to a single race in France the top three of the best races in France, Italy, Belgium and Switzerland in a *critérium des champions*. The race was superseded by the start of formal professional world championships in 1927 and it soon lost its prestige. The last was in 1931.

Chapter 3: 1927 – 1934

Pros (and others)
finally get their races

1927
First pro road championship

Pressure to hold a professional road championship had been building for seven years. Italy in particular wanted one and so did the French and Belgians. The best they got, in 1927, was a single race in which professionals and amateurs rode together with the best of each named champion.

The course was the newly opened Nürburgring car circuit in Germany, and legend insists that only the Italians Alfredo Binda and Costante Girardengo got up the toughest hills without walking.

Binda was a remarkable man. He won the Tour of Lombardy three times, Milan–San Remo twice, along with five Giros and 41 of its stages. He'd have won a sixth Giro had he not accepted the equivalent of first prize to stay away and give the others a chance. He and Girardengo were wildly better than the others but Binda was the stronger of the two. He dropped Girardengo with 30 kilometers left and gained a minute every four kilometers to win by 7 minutes 16 seconds.

Jean Aerts of Belgium was the best of the 33 amateurs, fifth at 11 minutes 51 seconds.

1928
By Georges, a record win

Binda and Girardengo never got over what happened in Germany. Like Fausto Coppi and Gino Bartali two decades later, they watched each other so closely that in the end they both got off in the 1928 champion-ship and were suspended for six months for "not having defended with faith and determination the prestige of Italian cycling."

The win at Budapest went instead to the Belgian, Georges Ronsse, thanks to the support of his team. While the Italians glared at each other, he went off and won by 19 minutes 43 seconds, a record. He won again in 1929.

1929
First cycle-ball championships

Nick Kaufman was German or Swiss. And sometimes he's described as American. Whoever he was, he noticed that bikes could be used for stunt riding which could in turn bring in paying crowds. In the pro-cess, he gave us two world championships, both administered by the UCI, which most of us don't know exist: cycle-ball and artistic cycling.

Cycle-ball probably started early in the 1900s. There are illustra-tions from that period of what looks like gentle afternoon exercise for the leisured classes. They already played polo on bicycles using mallets and a smaller ball, and Kaufman gave them a bigger ball to flip about with their bike or body. It became known as cycle-ball.

It's now an exclusively male game in which pairs of riders compete on fixed-wheel bikes with no brakes. While most don't realize it exists, it has cycling's most successful world champions. Jan and Jindřich Po-spíšil, brothers from Brno in what was then Czechoslovakia, won in 1965, then every year from 1968 to 1981, followed by every year from 1984 to 1988, winning their last gold medals when Jindřich was 46 and Jan 43.

Jindřich had already come second and third with his original part-ner, Jaroslav Svoboda, and the two brothers had come second in 1964.

Jindřich said: "It grew that we had a sixth sense. My brother could pass the ball when I couldn't see it and I'd know exactly where it would be. And I could rely on it."

The two started as circus stunt riders. They were training in a gym when they were spotted by a coach, Rudolf Hartha. He treated the boys as his sons, their father having died in May 1945 when the Russians freed Brno of the Germans. Jindřich said: "With his guidance, we won so much that there wasn't any more to do. The only way we could top it would have been to die on the field!" The brothers parted, Jan to Switzerland and Jindřich to coach in Czechoslovakia as well as working as a turner and grinder for a company making paper-making machines. Jindřich's granddaughter, Jana, came second in artistic cycling at a European junior championship.

1931
The wrong man wins

The 1931 track championships were in Denmark and the home crowd was thrilled that its man, Willie Falk Hansen, was in the final of the sprint. He was up against a Frenchman, Lucien Michard, and spectators naturally hoped for the best. It took some hoping, too, because Michard had won the four previous years and looked ready to win a fifth.

The starter set the two on their way and the chief judge, Alban Colignon, turned on the spot as he watched them slowly circling the track. Then they got to the last 200 meters and he checked who was where and settled his eyes on the line. It took no effort to see that Hansen, on the inside, had won. He was the new world champion, he announced.

But the crowd was oddly quiet and, then, angry. Even the Danes who'd have loved to see their man win had seen that he'd lost. The press, other officials, riders looking on…everyone knew it hadn't been Hansen. But Hansen was named champion of the world. Colignon had a sudden sinking feeling as he realized that Hansen and Michard had changed sides in the run-in to the finish and that he hadn't spotted it. Well, it was a classically foolish error but he was a modest man and he was happy to change his verdict.

The problem was that UCI's rules in those days insisted that a judge's decision was final and couldn't be changed. It was a way to stop riders and managers bickering in public as well as a way of raising the status of officials. Even if the judge knew he'd got it wrong, he still couldn't change it. But then the rule-makers hadn't thought of that.

And what happened next? Well, Hansen wore his rainbow jersey until the next championship and Michard had one run up to his own design and the two cleaned up with revenge matches all over Europe. Hansen went on to become a track director, particularly of six-day races. He died in Braşov, Romania, in 1978 and he's buried in Fårevejle,

Denmark. Michard won the French sprint championship ten times and seven Grand Prix de Paris. He stopped racing and began selling bikes bearing his name, in 1939 sponsoring a team with the Hutchinson tire company. He died largely unknown in 1985.

1931
Shambles on the road

The unintended drama of the 1931 track championship wasn't all that went wrong for the unfortunate Danes.

For years the British had begged the UCI to run the road championship against the clock. That was how things were done in Britain and the British hadn't had a medal since the race became a massed start. And then in 1931 they convinced the Danes and Denmark agreed to run the race as the British wanted. The British knew they had experience at riding against the clock and, with it, the easy superiority over other nations that they were prone to show in those days. And, of course, they'd taken all three medals last time.

They picked Freddy Frost, Len Cave and their almost unbeaten champion, Frank Southall, with F.T. Brown (initials were common in those days) as reserve, to ride the amateur race. The magazine *Cycling*, which reported little of what happened outside the island and often dismissed the entire Tour de France in four paragraphs, announced:

IF PERFECTLY FIT
Southall Will Win The World's
Road Championship,
predicts "The Loiterer."

Sadly for The Loiterer, things weren't done the way they were in England. Riders bunched up and got in each other's way, spectators' cars blocked the road, and nobody seemed to have heard of any rule about not taking shelter behind a faster rider. Southall himself sat on a wheel for 20 miles.

"The whole race was a disgrace," *Cycling*'s editor protested. "Crowds massed round the timekeeper, who couldn't see the riders. Numbers were called in one language and translated into others before they reached him. He missed Southall altogether but the British timed him at 5:6:26. The timekeeper left off the seconds and logged him at 5:6. At least five others got the wrong times and it was anybody's guess who'd done what. Southall ended up as 5:6:30."

The magazine's reporter sighed: "A time was recorded against a competitor's number given as 53. About that moment I had myself observed a rider crossing the line carrying the number 66 (Olmo, Italy). Three-quarters of an hour later an Italian delegate approached the timekeeper's table and for some moments completely monopolized the attention of the officials whilst he claimed that Olmo had arrived and that he had crossed the line 'one second after Henry Hansen.' After some minutes of heated discussion in French, Italian, Danish (and I could not resist saying a word, too), the time previously recorded against 53 was transferred to 66 and Olmo was listed second in the Amateur Road Championship of the world."

And then with a note of weary despair: "What happened to No. 53, T. Wanzenried, of Switzerland, I cannot say. He is not shown on the finishing list at all."

The interesting thing is that the report doesn't mention that Henry Hansen won. Giuseppe Olmo did indeed come second but you have to work out the rest for yourself.

The pro race, in which *Cycling* had no interest, was won by Learco Guerra of Italy. He didn't know, and *Cycling* wouldn't have cared, that two men watching him that day would create the unofficial world time trial championship as a result.

Frank Southall went on to be a professional long-distance record breaker and then to manage other professionals. He died in 1964. Hansen died in 1985 and Olmo in 1992.

1932
The unofficial time trial championship

The British idea that came unstuck in Denmark, when they wanted the world championship run their way, nevertheless provided the island with what it wanted. Not an official time trial championship but a race that had the same status. Even though its riders rarely took part and were always beaten when they did.

The idea of an unofficial world championship, the Grand Prix des Nations, was a sales gimmick thought up by a French journalist, Gaston Bénac. He worked for the evening paper *Paris-Soir*, which before the war had a circulation of two and a half million, Europe's largest. When its reporters got the result of Tour de France stages into print the night before Tour owner *L'Auto* could manage it, the Tour began starting and ending later each day to stop its happening.

Bénac had been in Copenhagen with a legendary cycling writer, Albert Baker d'Isy, who had worked for the erratic *L'Écho des Sports* before joining *Paris-Soir* the previous year. They concluded, as the British had, that for all the chaotic organization in Denmark, the Danes had seen the point: that a solo race against the clock was the purest of all. And such a thing was a novelty because there were no time trials in the Tour de France and only occasional French championships were run that way.

The two men hadn't been that interested in the amateur race that ended so disastrously, but they could see what Learco Guerra had achieved in riding 170 kilometers at 35.2 kilometers/hour. He had, after all, beaten their own French hope, Ferdinand Le Drogo. The two men saw a commercial possibility, one that *L'Auto* couldn't copy.

"What we need," Bénac told Baker d'Isy, "is a world championship, a world championship *contre la montre*, not just now and then but every year and right in the heart of Paris." Baker d'Isy thought up the name, the Grand Prix des Nations, a grand title for a revenge match for each year's world championship and a lot cheaper than an ordinary road race.

Baker d'Isy said he found the course. But so did René de Latour, a staff writer and later director of the Tour de l'Avenir. De Latour was the son of Franco-Belgian emigrants to New York who'd moved back to France when he was eight. The truth of who picked the route will never be known, not least because Baker d'Isy was, let us say, an inventive writer and because de Latour was never shy of boasting of his achievements and his closeness to the stars.

Both men agreed that Bénac said: "Take a day off and go out and find a course around 140 kilometers—and remember, no railway crossings!" Whoever it was, set out through the western suburbs of Paris along with a handful of local riders.

De Latour recalled: "With much searching of the maps, I got on the right track and after a few rides of inspection had found the course." It started near the Versailles château and ran round a triangle through Rambouillet, Maulette, St-Rémy-lès-Chevreuse, Versailles and Boulogne to finish on the Buffalo track where Henri Desgrange, the founder of the Tour de France, had become the world's first recognized hour-record holder in 1893.

The course had three hills and cobbles, and the last 40 kilometers went through the rolling woods of the Vallée de Chevreuse. Bénac had said 140 kilometers and it worked out at 142.

The problem that then arose was that Bénac and Baker d'Isy were keen, and the British—had they taken any notice—would have been keen, but the riders weren't. Denmark had been an unwelcome novelty that nobody wanted to repeat. Bénac and Baker d'Isy had to all but beg for riders. The first was Léon Le Calvez, a rider from the Breton heartland of French cycling who'd turned professional one Friday the previous summer so he could ride Bordeaux–Paris the next afternoon. He happened to drop in at *Paris-Soir* and found Bénac and Baker d'Isy rushing to sign him.

He remembered: "Bénac was complaining that French riders didn't want to ride because half of them were tired from the criteriums and the rest were scared. I gave in and discovered I wasn't such a bad *rouleur* after all." He came third to a plump but athletic Frenchman called Maurice Archambaud.

The following year, three hours before the start Le Calvez was in a restaurant with his team manager, Francis Pélissier, and his sponsor, the bike-maker Émile Mercier.

"I desperately need you to win," Mercier said, "because I need the publicity. Do it and I'll double your pay and give you 1,000 francs."

Encouraged, Le Calvez put in 16- and 24-spoke wheels, fitted 160 gram tubulars and used drilled-out chainrings on a bike that weighed less than 6 kilograms (13 pounds). He was going famously when he flatted on the climb at St-Rémy-lès-Chevreuse. Pélissier passed him in the team car as Le Calvez braked to a halt.

The rules said following cars were to be just that and that they weren't to pass under any pretext. Pélissier got out of the car and handed over a spare bike that had a bottle. The bike was fine: it was the bottle that was against the rules. Three days later, the French federation disqualified him.

He was as angry as everyone else. "The organizers were furious, because I'd already stopped when Francis passed me, and I didn't even notice the bottle," he said. "The people at *Paris-Soir* paid me what I'd

Les Woodland

have got for winning and they let me have the winner's cup. On the other hand, Monsieur Mercier didn't keep his promises. He'd got the publicity so he forgot to double my wage and he forgot the bonus. I was disheartened and next year I signed for Alcyon."

Le Calvez never again made the results. But Francis Pélissier brought about the greatest sequence of wins that the race knew. In 1953 a bundle of press cuttings came to him from the regional offices of Pélissier's new team sponsor, La Perle. The salesman in Normandy urged him to sign a 19-year-old before anyone else got to him. This kid, Jacques Anquetil, had been making a name for himself, he said.

Anquetil was aware of the three Pélissier brothers who'd so enlivened French cycling and he was flattered by the attention. A month later, Anquetil was leading the Grand Prix des Nations after 20 kilometers. He finished in just a shade less than 40 kilometers/hour. Unused to reporters, he said nervously: "It was no better than the end of Paris–Normandy", an amateur race in which he'd ridden the last 122 kilometers at 42 kilometers/hour and dropped the second man by nine minutes. And right now Anquetil was only a semi-professional.

Pélissier signed Anquetil as a full pro and waggled the cigarette in his mouth and said: "You ain't seen nothing yet." Anquetil won the Nations from 1953 to 1958, then again in 1961, 1965 and 1966. He was never beaten.

The oddest of odd riders over the years was the barrel-shaped Dutchman, Wim van Est. He got a contract in 1949 because he'd won a time trial in the Tour of Holland. He said:

> I'd never been to France. I went on the train to Paris and you had to take a little *carnet*, a little book for the bike for the customs. Everything, spare wheels everything, had to be in the book. And I didn't understand a word of French. *Niks!* And there was this Frenchman, great big mustache, and he was talking French and I was speaking Dutch and he was saying "*Parlez français!*" and I was shaking my head, "*Non, non*" and he couldn't understand me and I couldn't understand and, anyway, eventually I got away after an hour.
>
> And so then I had to get to a hotel. All I had was a card from the manager, Boulevard Magenta, Hôtel Angleterre, near the Gare du Nord. I'll take a taxi. And there was this

32

other Frenchman saying "*Pas bicyclette, pas bicyclette!*" and I was saying "*Ja, ja bicyclette!*" and we got it all taken to bits and I shoved it up in the front with the meter, and we were driving and driving and driving. Eiffel Tower, Place Pigalle, Place de Napoléon, the Sacré Coeur… and then the Eiffel Tower again.

I said: "We've already been by here! *Allez*, hotel, hotel!" And he was saying "*Piano, piano! Doucement!*" And by then I was getting really angry and I was banging on the window and shouting "*Godverdomme*, hotel!" I was in that taxi for an hour and a half, *godverdorie*!

And when I got there, there was the *garçon*, with a mustache and a blue apron, and I took the bike upstairs to my room. I mean, it was no chic hotel—just bare floors and old furniture. Well, by five o'clock the cleaning lady was complaining to the *patron* because the bike was dirty, because the previous day I'd won a race in Belgium and it had been raining all day. My leather saddle was soaked, my shoes were wet through, and so he said, the *patron*, "Let's take them down to the boiler room," and that was fine.

Next morning—the race was in the afternoon—I thought I'd go out training. So I put my tracksuit on and I went down to the boiler room, and I just about fell over with shock. He'd put my shoes on the top of the stove and leaned my bike up against it as well. And, *verdorie*, the saddle was about 12 centimeters long. Dried up. All crumpled up from drying out. And my shoes would have fitted a five-year-old. I didn't dare race. I thought I'd have to go back to the station.

Belgian journalists scoured Paris for secondhand shoes, and on a bike with only one brake—a cable snapped during the race—van Est came second to Charles Coste by only 13 seconds…after being misdirected at the entrance to the track.

Paris-Soir became reborn as *France-Soir* in 1944. It prospered at first but declined each time the owners changed. The Grand Prix des Nations moved to *L'Équipe*, itself the reborn *L'Auto*, which had been closed after the war. The Nations, however, was never the same.

There were other time trials and organizing a race so close to Paris was difficult. In 1972 it moved to Cannes and then again to Dieppe. The distance dropped to 75 kilometers and the race vanished after 2004.

Ten years earlier, the UCI had begun its own, now official, world time trial championship.

1933
The playboy champion

Selectors rarely have an easy time. Nobody praises them if they get it right. And then they get it in the ear if their man dares to come second rather than first. But now and then they make really odd decisions. In 1933 France, for instance, they reckoned that any man who could win the Tour de France would be too puffed out to ride the world championship. So they left out their star man, Georges Speicher.

Now, Georges was a colorful man. He was happy-looking with slim legs, wavy hair and heavy eyelids and the laconic look you get from going to nightclubs. Which, having been left out of the world championship team, is where he went. He was disappointed, yes, but he'd been paid a hefty bonus by Alcyon, who'd sold 845,045 bikes just on the strength of his Tour win, and that had been a consolation.

Sadly for the selectors, one of their team, Paul Chocque, dropped out ill at the last moment. (That wasn't the end of his troubles; he died in 1949 after a crash in a motor-paced race at the Parc des Princes.) And overcoming the hurt pride caused by the thousands about to say "We told you so," they went looking for Georges. They tried him at home and they tried his friends and finally they went round the bars and clubs of Pigalle. And there, late at night, they finally found him, probably with a boozy grin on his face.

And what happened? Georges went home, got his bike and clothes, drove to the car racing circuit at Montlhéry…and won the world championship. He looked bleary and just a little tubby when he arrived and the team's manager asked him only to set a good speed at the start and set the tone for the rest of the team. So he rode off and, after 50 kilometers, attacked to make the others chase and show who had legs and who not. But the opposition knew Speicher hadn't much trained and even less raced since the

Tour and they let him go. Despite being in a bar half the night, he won by five minutes, the first Frenchman to become professional road champion and the first rider to win the Tour and the world championship in the same year.

1934
The youngest winner

They've done it up since then but the Sportpaleis beside the highway north out of Antwerp used to be a real sight. It sat big, brick and glum as a bus station in an unsurfaced parking lot that became a mire at the first fall of Belgian rain. It had an advertisement painted on an outside wall for a newspaper that had gone out of business years earlier. And the ice rink inside the bike track made the building so cold at night that riders sometimes wore tracksuit tops during the six-day there.

But it reeked of atmosphere. The walls were stained by decades of cigarette smoke puffed by bike fans who knew what they were watching and flocked there time after time for a good night out among the wheels. And you could guess that where you spilled your beer was where some bygone champion had spilled his long before you.

The man who for many years sold that beer, in a bar just inside the big doors, was a tall and heavily built man with a boyish smile and a spreading waist. His name was Karel Kaers and he was the youngest man ever to win the world professional championship of the world.

He was born in June 1914 in Vosselaar, where a road is named after him. He began on the track, where he won the national junior sprint. And he was still better known abroad as a track rider when Belgium included him in its road team for the world championship in the Scheibenholz park in Leipzig in 1934.

The circuit was flat, which suited Kaers, who weighed 85 kilograms and struggled on hills. It was also a comparatively short race, at 225 kilometers. When he used his track sprint to beat Learco Guerra after a long break, he was dismissed as an opportunist who'd won a championship no more demanding than a Belgian street race. He had simply clung to Guerra, folk said, an excellent solo rider who'd won the world championship in Denmark when it had been run against the clock. No wonder Kaers had won.

Les Woodland

He came by Guerra with 300 meters to go. Guerra tried to come back by him on the left but Kaers squeezed him up against the barriers. He protested but the referees decided against him.

De Latour reflected on claims that Kaers had had an easy win because the circuit was so undemanding: "What would have happened if the race had been on a hilly course? The answer was simply that he would not have been picked to ride. Not for a fortune could he have climbed a col in the Alps or Pyrenees. But, on a flat or slightly undulating road—my! I have seen few riders to touch him."

One of Kaers' many achievements was his discovery of a young Rik van Steenbergen. He was, de Latour said, the first to put van Steenbergen's feet into toe-clips. The two met during the Occupation and Kaers loaned and even gave him his bike bits so that he could race when the shelves of bike shops were bare.

"The diver who finds a pearl is just a lucky chap," Kaers said. "He is no more gifted than the one who goes through a pile of oysters and finds none. I didn't invent Rik van Steenbergen; he came to light on his own."

After the war, he also discovered the Dutchman, René Pijnen, a star of six-day races as well as a professional road rider.

Chapter 4: 1946 – 1953

The pre-war racers dominate; Coppi gets one last big win

1946
The man who had to flee the country

Tradition has it that there's sympathy for the underdog. To have tried but failed, to have given your best but come away bloodied, all admirable notions. What we don't so often feel is such anger that the man who comes second has to flee the country. But so it was for Rik van Steenbergen. Well, actually, he came third, but the rest of it's true.

The first world championship after the war was in Zürich, a sensible choice because Switzerland had been neutral and old enemies in the crowd would surely not be so impolite as to fight in front of the sober Swiss.

The last professional champion before the war was Marcel Kint of Belgium, nicknamed the Black Eagle because of his beak nose and dark hair and black jersey. The amateur champion that same year was Hans Knecht of Switzerland. Now both were to ride against each other as professionals. Hearts were with Kint. There was admiration for the gritty, unrelenting way he rode and there was a romantic wish that the world could restart after the war where it had been before, that all that went between the two could be forgotten. To see Kint back in a rainbow jersey, eight years later, would do just that.

And for a while it looked like happening. Kint impressed throughout the race and then broke away alone in the last hour. He looked sure of bringing the dream to life. But then his own team-mate, van Steenbergen, set off in chase with Knecht on his wheel. They caught

Les Woodland

the tiring Kint and Knecht rode away on a cobbled hill to beat both of them.

It smelled of rotten fish. Why would van Steenbergen chase his teammate? Why would he so readily take Knecht with him? And if van Steenbergen finished third of three even as the world's best road sprinter, was that not because he was too ashamed to pass Kint? Or maybe money had changed hands.

Years later at his home outside Antwerp, van Steenbergen blamed it on bad luck, often talking of himself in the third person as though detaching himself from the story.

> Just as ever, there was no agreement between the Belgian riders who they were going to ride for. Since nothing had been settled I thought, right, I'll take my chance. On the last lap Marcel Kint, the best rider in the world in those days, he attacked and took 25 seconds. Then I went and on my wheel I had the Swiss, Knecht. I couldn't get him off.

> I had to pull out everything, everything, everything to get up to Kint. I swung over for the other guy, but he wouldn't come through. He just sat on my wheel. One kilometer from the line, I finally got up to Marcel Kint. At that moment, the guy on my wheel jumped away. I couldn't react, nor would Kint. We were beaten, the two best riders in the world. Beaten. Here in Belgium, they were all convinced that we had sold out to Knecht.

> Never in 22 years have I sold a world championship. Anyway, the people called me everything. Then there was pressure on the Belgian federation that van Steenbergen should not be selected again for the world championship. I wasn't to be picked any more. It got so bad that my manager, van Buggenhout, said: "Stay away for 14 days, keep out of Belgium." It was a great scandal…

> Well, against my personal taste, I decided to ride the Tour de France, in 1949, just to win a stage and get my place back in the world championship team. I won the Tour of Limburg, I won the Flèche Wallonne, and still they wouldn't pick me. So my manager, van Buggenhout, said you've got to ride the

Tour de France. I won the last stage—the 300 kilometers to
Paris in the Parc des Princes. That was the breakthrough. It
was settled and I was picked for the world's. That rather put
the pressure on me to win, didn't it?

The historian Alain Rivolla says: "Despite his profile and being
called an eagle, Marcel Kint wasn't bitter. Once he'd got over the defeat,
he seemed to form a real friendship with Rik van Steenbergen, and
they made a formidable pair together on the road and on the track,
where they won seven races in three years. But, alas, Marcel Kint's best
years were wasted because of the Occupation and at 32 years old he'd
seen his last chance of winning a world championship slip by him."

And van Steenbergen? He did win that world championship in
1949, outsprinting Ferdi Kübler and Fausto Coppi.

1947
Last pounce of the cat

Jef Scherens used to crouch on his bike and then spring. Since he
came from the university city of Leuven, a bidon's throw into the
Dutch-speaking half of Belgium, they called him *Poeske*, Dutch for
"kitten" or "little cat."

This pouncing cat won the world sprint championship every year
from 1932 to 1937. He lost to the academic-looking Arie van Vliet of
Holland in 1938 and was about to meet him again in the final in 1939
when war broke out that very day. The race was abandoned and Scherens was credited with second place.

He was beaten early in 1946 but in 1947 in Paris he won his seventh
championship, beating Louis Gérardin of France and another Frenchman, Georges Senfftleben. But for the war, he would probably be the
world's most successful sprinter and not Japan's Koichi Nakano.

Scherens was a favorite with crowds because he was an entertainer
as much as a racer. His favorite trick was to win in only the last ten
meters, when it looked that all was lost. Pascal Sergent wrote: "After 75
years, it's hard to imagine today just how popular Jef Scherens was. In
Belgium and elsewhere, he was nothing less than an institution. Thousands of people would turn out every time he appeared."

He retired at a track meeting in Brussels in 1951, when he was 42.

Les Woodland

1948
The problems of Captain Grumpy

The sport of cycling can be petty. It's an enclosed world that lives only so one man can be better than another. So, for all the smiles and back slaps, each is out to do the other down. And if one wins more, or is more popular, he earns more and the other gets less. It is a commercial enterprise fought not through advertisements but on the road with aching legs and wounded pride.

The civil war after the second world war was between two Italians, the aging Gino Bartali and his young pretender, a frail and beak-nosed man called Fausto Coppi. They couldn't be more different. Differences were exaggerated by reporters who had to draw mental sketches in the day before television but differences there were.

Bartali looked like a fleshy pizza chef, with a bulbous nose, a short squat body and a face lined with the effort of work. He was deeply religious in a suffocatingly observant country and it was in him that the devout and the conservative saw themselves. He was also notoriously grumpy, which made them warm to him even more. His commonest expression was: "It's all a mess; let's start over again." His nickname was Ginettaccio, which is hard to translate but corresponds with Captain Grumpy.

Coppi, on the other hand, was lean and heron-like; no more a city slicker than Bartali but nevertheless the emblem of a more progressive Italy, less believing, more outward-looking, the vanguard of a society that in time rode Vespas and crowded into cars slightly smaller than themselves. He wasn't often any happier than Bartali; in Pierre Chany's words, he had "an air of perpetual sadness."

What made the friction greater was that Coppi had been hired to help Bartali, only to belittle him. The elder resented being shamed and deposed, the younger resented being prince to a failing king.

And so the two men came to ride in the same team, not over the several weeks of the Tour de France—which in those days was for national rather than commercial teams and during which the ebb and flow of fortune could disguise much of what was going on—but in the world championship. Two lives, two social factions, two contradicting ambitions, were to be crammed together for seven hours. And at the end, one or the other or neither would be champion of the world.

Cycling's World Championships

The distance between the two began with mutual sniping in the press. Then Coppi stayed in a private house the night before the race rather than share a hotel with the rest of the team and risk meeting Bartali. Alfredo Martini, one of the riders hired to help the stars, recalled: "Gino arrived and all seemed pretty normal. The issue was that he and Coppi weren't communicating with each other at all by now. We were all used to that but this time it was so strained between them that Coppi took himself off altogether. He figured that if he stayed away from the hotel there'd be less tension."

The race that year was in Holland, near the appealing city of Valkenburg in the hilly south-eastern province of Limburg. The name of the town means Falcon Hill, which gives an idea of the topography. The circuit, however, was largely flat, although with repeated climbs of the Cauberg to break things up. Which it certainly would after no less than 266 kilometers.

The story behind the race was that Bartali had had the edge in the Tour de France and that Coppi had won so little since the start of the season that it was rumored his sponsor, Bianchi, was wondering why it was spending so much time and money on him.

It was too bad that one man should do better than the other, for one to be crowned and the other dismissed. And so the two spent the day joined at the hip. When Coppi went into the changing room, then Bartali went too. There's little reason to think that Bartali was naive in these things but he was convinced, rightly, that Coppi was a devotee of the pill bottle. Perhaps, if Bartali was there to see, Coppi would have to restrain himself. After all, as Coppi said in retirement, he did take drugs.

"But only when necessary," he added when a television presenter put the question.

"And how often was that?"

"Almost always."

Bartali worried what Coppi would do. They may have been rivals but they were also now in the same team.

"Don't worry," Coppi replied coldly, "wherever you go, I'll go too."

And so Coppi and Bartali went slower and slower, each accompanied by puzzled and despairing team riders who had nothing to gain but the bonus they'd been promised if either man won. If one tried anything, the other followed. To the howls of Italians who'd made a long and difficult journey north and the many who'd moved to Belgium or Holland for work—the brick-works and mines of northern Europe employed thousands of Italians hoping to send money home—the two had lost ten minutes on the rest before they conceded on the penultimate lap and climbed off on a stretch of road with few spectators.

"I told you," Coppi sneered. "Wherever you went, I'd go too. If you're going back to the hotel, I'll even follow you there." The two broke into a furious row, to the delight of newsreel cameramen who'd found them and were happy to record the moment. Things became still better for them that evening when fans shouted and hurled eggs and vegetables outside the team hotel, disgusted at the men they'd wanted to see dominate the world.

In the end, the title went to Briek Schotte of neighboring Belgium, who outsprinted Apo Lazaridès with another Frenchman, Lucien Teisseire, third. Only ten riders were counted in.

There was no great happiness in the offices of the Italian cycling federation. Saying euphemistically that there'd been "a lack of willingness" to compete, it suspended both for six months, then reduced it two months. To be precise, it said: "In the professional world championship on the road, they forgot the honor that was granted to them to uphold Italian prestige. They thought only of their personal rivalry and abandoned the competition, arousing the unanimous criticism of all sportsmen."

In the end they scrapped the ban completely, recognizing that their own team officials were also to blame. They had appointed a federation employee called Lugari as manager and the job had been beyond him. And they realized that a sport with neither Coppi nor Bartali would be stale beer. It told both they could race again but that in future they'd better mind their step.

Coppi never spoke publicly of that day. But Bartali wrote: "I had my share of the blame in what happened. And Fausto was constrained by commercial orders he couldn't get out of. Because Bianchi wanted me to lose and he was a Bianchi employee."

Or as Martini put it: "Every time one or the other won, the stakes got higher. You'd also got the commercial interests of Legnano and Bianchi at play. Had Bartali won the rainbow jersey so soon after the

Cycling's World Championships

Tour, it would have done wonders for Legnano's sales and, by extension, it would have been disastrous for Bianchi. There was even speculation that Coppi hadn't even wanted to come to Holland but Bianchi obliged him to go, to stop Bartali winning."

Just how bitter the rivalry was emerged years later. Luciano Maggini was a team man that day in Holland. Coppi had wanted him as a domestique but Lugari had told him two days before the race, having looked at the circuit, that he was to ride for Bartali instead. Maggini was no fool, though, and recognized he stood his own chance if Coppi and Bartali were self-possessed. And so he attacked from the start, then again when he was caught, and then a last time. Which was when his chain snapped and he had to stand by the roadside and watch the field ride by.

In time he got a spare bike, which didn't fit him, chased back to the leaders and finally finished 6 minutes 40 seconds behind Schotte, crossing the line fourth with a flat front tire. That evening in the hotel, he went to look at his original bike, a Wilier. And the chain had been sawed through.

Decades passed without his knowing who had sabotaged him. And then:

> Twenty-five years later, Bartali called me. There was to be a meeting [of guys from] the golden age, in Rome. Come along, he said, lots of friends will be there. I agreed. When the dinner was almost over, I went to Gino and I quietly asked him: "So many years have passed but I've always had a nagging question: do you know who cut my chain at Valkenburg?"
>
> He looked at me with wide and unbelieving eyes as if I was joking. When he understood that I had never solved that issue, he whispered: "Pinella Golden Pliers."
>
> "Coppi's mechanic?"
>
> "Yes," he said.
>
> "Wow," I said. "Are you sure?"
>
> "Yes," he said. "I swear." With the storm brewing between the two, even the mechanic tried to limit Bartali by damaging me in a way.

Les Woodland

1948
Harris in high dudgeon

The track championships in Amsterdam were an anticlimax, mainly because they came only two weeks after the Olympic Games in London. World amateur championships had far lower status than the Games and the largely empty spaces around the never-ending track that circuited a soccer pitch demonstrated that. And the crowd must have wondered whether it was disappointed that not one of the defending champions managed to keep his title or if it was pleased to see the rise of new or at least unexpected talent. Those denied gold medals included Coppi in the pursuit and the Briton, Reg Harris, in the amateur sprint.

The UCI had ruled that all the amateur sprints had to be finished in one day rather than two. That meant racing on into the evening, no lessons having been learned from the London Olympics which had ended in such darkness that the crowd could no longer see the racing.

Harris said in his biography: "I defeated Scharndorff [of Denmark] in the first round of the semifinals, which boosted my morale. But when I wanted to use maximum effort in the second round, the strength just was not there and I lost. I gave the decider everything I had got, with the result that it was declared a photo finish.

"When the photograph was quickly examined, it was discovered that the light had been so bad that it was impossible to tell from it who had won. The judges' only course of action was to declare it a dead heat and call for another decider to be run."

The power was no longer there and Harris lost by half a wheel. He went home with the bronze medal, "feeling utterly miserable." It was disappointment at Amsterdam that persuaded Harris to turn professional. The championship winner was the baby-faced 19-year-old Italian, Mario Ghella, who'd beaten Harris in the Olympics two weeks earlier. Little more was ever heard of him.

The professional favorite was the home star, Arie van Vliet, then 32 years old. Like all the older riders, his career had been broken by war. He reestablished Dutch pride by beating Louis Gérardin of France in the sprint.

Harris became upset when the Dutch sprinter, Jan Derksen, remembered that Harris had just one tactic: a *krachtexplosie*. When the power exploded, he said, it was awful for everyone close by but after that there was nothing left. This was the same man—Harris—who flung tea over a reporter who asked how much he had been paid to lose a championship.

Harris' life was a story you couldn't invent—although, as you'll see later, he had a good go at it. He was nearly burned alive in a tank in the North Africa during the war. He was discharged and sent home. He was rammed in his sports car as he headed for a meeting in London. His back was broken and his legs paralyzed. Just months later, he became professional champion of the world in Copenhagen in 1949, beating Derksen.

Harris made a good living out of rivalry with van Vliet. He identified van Vliet's weakness as "never having been out in a cape and sou'wester and ridden in the rain for eight hours." Van Vliet's background was middle class but Harris came from what Harry Traynor, Raleigh's press officer, called "a cotton mill and cloth cap background." Harris dominated world championships so much—winning in 1949, 1950, 1951 and 1954, and coming third in 1953 and second in 1956— that the UCI changed to three-man finals to stop him. Or that was how Harris saw it, anyway.

He died aged 72 in June 1992 after a heart attack while cycling the previous day.

Amsterdam was the first championship with a South African team. J.J. Brand, Ginger Olivier and Eddie Scholtz rode but left no record. It was a brief venture into world cycling because in 1960 South Africa, which had a cycling federation for whites, another for blacks and a third for "coloreds", was excluded from world sport.

1950
First cyclo-cross world championship

The first world cyclo-cross championship in 1950 wasn't quite the first. There had been what amounted to a world championship, the Critérium International, since 1924.

The 1924 Critérium was in the woods of St-Cucufa, west of Paris. It included a spectacular descent into the *Trou du Diable*—the devil's hole—wide enough for only one rider at a time. The winner was Gaston Degy, a Frenchman born in Belgium, who also rode the Tour de

France in 1914 and then every summer from 1921 to 1924. He went on to become an excitable manager of the world's top track riders.

Stars frequently took part, including Charles and Francis Pélissier, Sylvère Maes and Georges Ronsse. The sport took off because Octave Lapize said he had won the Tour in 1910 thanks to cross-country racing the previous winter.

The status of the Critérium assured sponsorship and it became the Grand Prix Martini and a battleground between the Tour winner, Jean Robic, and another Frenchman, Roger Rondeaux. Their rivalry extended to the road, reaching the point at which Robic rode up beside Rondeaux and said: "If you let me beat you today, I'll never bother you in a cyclo-cross again."

The GP Martini became the formal world championship in 1950, moving to the Bois de Vincennes, also outside Paris, and Robic won it. He had also won the Critérium in 1947, the year he won the Tour. Robic hadn't intended to ride the championship, though. He was a disagreeable man but he stuck to his word and he explained to Achille Joinard, the president of the French federation, that he couldn't ride for France for fear of beating Rondeaux. Joinard couldn't talk him out of it and the problem was solved only when he asked Rondeaux to tell Robic that their deal could be suspended for this one race.

Until 1966, cyclo-cross was regarded more as winter larking about than a serious race, and there was no distinction between amateurs and professionals. Then there were separate races for each until, in 1994, the UCI abandoned the distinction and held just a single senior championship. The first junior world championship was in 1976 and the first for women in 2000.

The most successful rider was Erik De Vlaeminck of Belgium, who won in 1966 and then every year from 1968 to 1973. The second best is André Dufraisse, of France, who won five championships in a row and two silver and four bronze medals, all between 1951 and 1963. Belgium is by far the most successful nation in the team competition.

1950
First world cup

The idea of finding a global super-hero—or at any rate a European super-hero, because the sport for a long time looked neither west from

Cycling's World Championships

Calais nor anywhere beyond the Black Sea—had always been obvious. The trouble was that for decades it was hard to get to races that riders *did* want to start, let alone those that the sport's administrators felt they *ought* to have a go at.

The travel problems had hardly improved by the end of the second world war but social need had. Finding races that would bring together former enemies would be good for the world as well as, it has to be said, for the sales of newspapers.

The position when peace came to the world in 1945 was that there were long-established races, known as classics but which attracted largely domestic fields. If riders rode outside their own country, it was only because they lived close to a border and it suited them or because, as Belgian riders often did for instance, they rode for sponsors in another land and had to race there. Since an Italian or Spanish sponsor was unlikely to be as interested in sales in Germany or Holland, assuming it had any at all, as it was in stimulating business at home, it followed that it was rare for riders to travel abroad more than occasionally and then only with much adventure.

The situation was so marked that for many years riders were allowed to have different sponsors in different countries. That was seen as a way of lessening the cost for each sponsor, of improving the situation for each rider, and a way of attracting riders to compete in more than one country. But these rare foreign visitors were just summer birds and the three main sports newspapers—*L'Équipe* in France, *Les Sports* in Belgium and *La Gazzetta dello Sport*, the newspaper that founded the Giro d'Italia—wanted more. Their readers were nationalistic, certainly, but it was getting tiring, writing about the same circus of riders and teams.

"I've got a good idea," someone said. "Why don't we have a competition for the rider who does best all through the season? It'd be good for the sport."

The newspapermen round the table nodded. "Good for the sport" meant "good for circulation."

"What?" someone asked. "As well as the world championship?"

Well, yes. That was just one day, one race. If a Frenchman won, that was good for *L'Équipe* but nobody else sold any more copies. And no more copies meant no increase in advertising rates. But a race every couple of weeks, to create and then sustain suspense, would be going back to the good old days when newspapers invented long races knowing that fans who bought the paper before the start would have to buy one during and after the competition as well.

Then someone said: "But only one person can win? What's the difference?"

To which the answer was: "The difference is that the lead can change many times, and there will be many little world championships, in all our countries. We can promote our heroes and when the winner will be not only a true champion, wherever he comes from, but our readers will have seen on their own roads."

And so the Challenge Desgrange-Colombo was born, named after the founders of the Tour and the Giro. Both those races would count and so would Milan–San Remo, the Tours of Flanders and Lombardy, Paris–Tours, the Waalse Pijl, Paris–Roubaix and Paris–Brussels. Others such as Liège–Bastogne–Liège were added later.

It was an immediate success. Italians began to compete in France and Belgium. Frenchmen such as Louison Bobet got themselves separate sponsors in Italy. The first results sheet in 1950 was a *Who's Who* of cycling: Ferdi Kübler, Fiorenzo Magni, Hugo Koblet, Fausto Coppi and Gino Bartali.

Inevitably, there was a row. This was cycling, so how could it be otherwise? There were the usual commercial disagreements, of course, but also the discovery that the trophy could be won by riders who did well throughout the season without always starring. In modern times, that produced riders like Paolo Bettini, for instance. In that earlier era, it meant that Fred De Bruyne won in 1956, 1957 and 1958. He could win Milan–San Remo, Liège–Bastogne–Liège and the Tour of Flanders but he was never better than 17th in the Tour.

Italy and France disagreed over how long the competition should run and so nobody ran it at all. That left a gap for commerce to fill and in 1960 the Pernod company, which made an aniseed aperitif which for a few more years wasn't to fall foul of a French ban on alcohol advertising that had come from rampant alcoholism in the country, ran the Prestige Pernod on races in France. When nobody restored the Challenge Desgrange-Colombo, it did it itself and called it the Super Prestige Pernod. The original Prestige Pernod continued but just for French riders.

Cycling's World Championships

The first three in 1961 were Jacques Anquetil, Raymond Poulidor and Rik van Looy. No longer was there room for a "does his best" rider of the De Bruyne mold. Not once was the Super Prestige won by an outsider. Eddy Merckx won every year from 1969 to 1975. For a comparison between him and later riders, a game that fans always play, it's worth remembering that Merckx won the Super Prestige in 1971 with twice the points of the second, third, fourth and fifth riders. Not twice any one of their points…all their points combined. And he won the Tour five times.

In the end Paris banned drinks advertising, which ended Anquetil's St-Raphaël team and Jan Janssen's Pelforth. The Super Prestige Pernod lasted a little longer thanks to legal maneuvering and geography but it ended after Stephen Roche in 1987 and Charly Mottet in 1988. After which cycling took the championship unto itself and started the World Cup. Many say its scope isn't as wide, that it doesn't produce the same champions, or that the same champions aren't there to produce. The way the competition has changed with the years suggests that the UCI recognizes that.

But to win a season-long competition, a summer-long stage race, demands a rider better than all the others and better for a longer time. Many say that it would be the way to find a true world champion, that it is fairer and arithmetically superior. And others say that that is precisely its shortcoming and that there's nothing like the cut and thrust of a single race with a national anthem and a rainbow jersey at the end.

The row isn't ever likely to end. Not for a while, anyway. Because the more we talk about it, the more we prove that those three newspapers of years ago were right.

1951
The rough with the smooth

No two men could have been more different than Hugo Koblet and Ferdi Kübler. They came from the same German-speaking region of Switzerland but otherwise from different worlds. Koblet was an educated, sophisticated man who pedaled so smoothly and looked so dashingly handsome that the French singer, Jacques Grello, gave him a nickname that stuck: *le pédaleur de charme*. Kübler was wild, full of mouth, extravagant and gauche.

Les Woodland

In 1951, Koblet won the Tour de France, partly through a long, lone break to Agen on the day before the race reached the Pyrenees. Typically, he picked a comb from his pocket and spruced himself up before crossing the line.

Kübler never bothered to spruce himself up. He rode and spoke with wild enthusiasm and sweated and swore and foamed at the mouth. Another difference was that Koblet faded fast and died young, possibly by suicide. He peaked and he declined spectacularly, even between the Tour and the world championship in Varese in the heart of the lake district of northern Italy.

Koblet had lost the pursuit championship in Milan against another roadman, Antonio Bevilacqua. Which encouraged Kübler to think that he may be not just the best Swiss on the start line but maybe even the best in the world.

The Italians, of course, were on home ground. They had to start without Fausto Coppi, who was at home with a fever, and that left them the aging Gino Bartali, the unpopular Fiorenzo Magni, who said himself that he was tired after too much racing, and the new pursuit champion, Bevilacqua.

Nobody knows just how many stood by the roadside to see how they were going to sort out a difficult choice. Some say 800,000, others even a million. However many there were, they watched the world's best ride 24 laps of a circuit which the French press called "tormented". And they saw Italy get Bevilacqua into the first real break, after 74 kilometers. There were nine of them: Bevilacqua, Giuseppe Minardi also of Italy, Kübler, and Gerrit Voorting, Wout Wagtmans and Henk Faanhof of Holland, Jos De Feyter from Belgium, the naturalized Frenchman Attilio Redolfi, and Erwin Schwarzer, a lesser rider from Switzerland.

They got five minutes' lead, losing Redolfi and Faanhof in the process. Magni saw the risk and chased for 50 kilometers to catch them. Koblet tried to follow and so did Bartali, but they were too weak, too late. They did get to two minutes, though, which served only to seal their fate as the leaders rode still faster. The Italians attacked in turn to force the rest to chase, tiring themselves while Magni rode on their wheels. But if Magni was already weary before the race set off, he was even more tired now after close on two hours of chasing alone. Kübler could see that. He waited until the last 500 meters and cut the rest at the knees, just the second-ever Swiss road champion since Hans Knecht in 1946. He was already loosening his toe straps as he crossed the line, a bike length's gap ahead of Magni.

"I think I got my season just right," he said at the finish. "You can't ride everything. You have to know how to choose. I chose not to ride the Tour and I noticed that the big names who did ride it weren't there today, with the exception of Bartali and Magni."

Kübler rode in an era when travel was hard and races were harder. His sponsor for many years was the Tebag company, which sold car tires and made bikes as a sideline. Not every Swiss then could afford a car and Tebag wanted to cover the market. It was an era when training was no more scientific than riding even more kilometers than the next guy and then racing. Fritz Dietsche, one of the founders of Tebag, took that further and persuaded his riders not to drive.

"Cars are not for racing cyclists," he used to say.

1953
Coppi's last stand

There was a sickly moment in a newsreel just before the 1953 world championship when Marina Coppi read a letter begging her father to come back home as world champion. It shows the reverence in which the now fading hero—he was 34—was still held. And it gives credence to reports that Italian fans got down on their knees and kissed the road where Coppi passed.

But the discord in her parents' life was already well established. Marina may not have known it or seen the significance, but pictures had begun appearing of Coppi with another woman, sometimes named and sometimes not. Italian papers dropped deep hints, foreign newspapers hadn't caught on to who she was, but she was an open secret among other riders. It would never make a whiff of scandal now, but in Italy of the 1950s it was enough to have Coppi excommunicated from the Roman Catholic church.

It was with that cloud growing over him that Coppi went to Lugano, at the top of a little Swiss panhandle that drops down into Italy. To many it was known as the Crespera circuit, after the climb the championship was going to take. The hill is just 1.7 kilometers long but it averages 7.8 percent and, after 20 times, it was going to tell. And in those days it was still cobbled.

Coppi had never been comfortable in world championships and the preposterous slow bicycle bout with Gino Bartali at Valkenburg was still a sore. His view was that world championship courses were always too easy for him. Like Eddy Merckx two decades later, his style was to ride everyone else off his wheel. And that couldn't happen on what Coppi considered easy courses.

On the other hand, a career becomes great only if it includes a world championship and Coppi was as aware of his place in history as any other star. So, being truthfully persuaded that this was his last chance, he trained and rested for a month rather than make himself richer by riding appearance races all round Italy. That training included laps of the Lugano circuit with the novice professional, Michele Gismondi, who'd agreed to be Coppi's foot soldier for the race.

That loyalty was important. The Italian national team was as divided as Belgium's. And although this time Bartali wouldn't be riding, there were many who had to be picked who saw their own chances first and then the doing down of Coppi next. The man had many enemies, through jealousy, past slights, the sort of everyday problems that come up in any hard, commercial sport in which emotions are easily frayed by tiredness.

The debate over who would ride for whom and when and why went on late. But the hot air was wasted because Charly Gaul attacked after just 20 kilometers and Coppi went with him to end further debate, and Ferdi Kübler and Raphaël Géminiani joined in as well. And to make the point even more acutely, Coppi attacked the twelfth time up the Crespera climb, riding so hard that only a Belgian, Germain Derycke, could match him. But either Derycke could do no better or he knew he only had to be escorted round the rest of the race by the man most likely to win it and perhaps he could nip by at the end and beat him.

Well, we all have our dreams. And Derycke's ended when Coppi rode away from him the next time up the Crespera, taking an erratic path to make the Belgian lose his rhythm and then crack. And Derycke cracked on the bend at the top.

The days had yet to come when riders flamboyantly threw both arms in the air as they won. In the 1950s, the wave was more an acknowledgment of the crowd's applause and, accordingly, Coppi lifted one hand as he crossed the line 6 minutes 16 seconds ahead of Derycke and seven and a half minutes before another Belgian, Stan Ockers. He went to the podium not with his wife but his lover. His wife was also there but in the background. The two women met, perhaps for the first time, after the race. Life for all three of them was never going to be the same again.

As Jean-Paul Ollivier wrote in his biography of Coppi: "The flash bulbs spluttered. In Italy next day, the photo of Coppi the adulterer appeared. Today the crowd cried but tomorrow it turned against him and Giulia was shouted down as the 'sinner' too quick to meddle in the life of their champion. Some journalists, though, didn't want to believe it and in glowing terms they reported only the great success he had brought to the cycling world."

Lo Sport, for instance, wrote: "Today again there are ill-intentioned people of bad faith who are claiming the most stupid and unbelievable things. Let's stop this campaign of lies and look up to this great athlete who's made us so happy."

Lo Sport was in the minority but there was no doubt that Coppi had made a nation happy, and specifically that section of the nation there that day to see him win. As well as the story of fans kissing the road, it's also said that so many Italians were, shall we say, boisterously noisy as they crossed back into Italy that Customs gave up trying to make them pay tax on the wine and chocolate they brought back with them and just lifted the barrier.

Nobody knew it then but that world championship of 1953 was one of the last big races that Coppi won. The end was on its way.

Chapter 5: 1954 – 1966

Women get their own race;
a surprise English winner

1954
Man of steel

Charles Pélissier was the weakest of the brothers who dominated French cycling of the 1930s but he was the most handsome and certainly the most literate. He was talking to Louison Bobet during the 1954 Tour, for the weekly magazine, *Miroir Sprint*, and then ended his moments with the race leader with the advice: "In your condition, there's nobody around who could beat you. Forget about the criteriums after the Tour, or most of them, and start training to become champion of the world."

No Frenchman had won the professional road championship for nearly 20 years, not since Antonin Magne in Berne, in 1936. And right now, Antonin Magne happened to be Bobet's team manager. He knew his boy was at the top of world cycling but he reckoned he needed still more. He agreed with Pélissier. So the thought started turning. And towards the end of the year, Bobet was on the start line at Solingen, a steel town south of the industrial Ruhr.

He and his agent, the gangster-lookalike Daniel Dousset, recognized that the greatest challenge came from Fausto Coppi, who had not ridden the Tour and would be fresher for it. Predictably, Coppi attacked with 50 kilometers to go. He caught the early leaders with Fritz Schaer of Switzerland, Charly Gaul of Luxembourg, and three Frenchmen: Bobet, Jacques Anquetil and Jean Forestier. Bobet was the other favorite, Schaer had won the Tour's first sprinters' jersey, Gaul was a climber, Anquetil a time trialist who loathed Bobet and would do little to help him, and Forestier was good enough to become *maillot jaune* and points winner in the Tour three years later.

Bobet attacked ten times and dropped Anquetil and Forestier. The rain poured and puddled. Coppi lost concentration on a wet descent and crashed into Gaul, demolishing him as well. Which left Bobet with Schaer.

He waited for the Balhaüsen hill, then attacked hard. Schaer clung to his wheel. They passed the feeding station and there Paul Delaye, the French mechanic, saw spokes were breaking in Bobet's back wheel. There are many versions of what happened next. Some say Delaye was in a car, others that he jumped on a bike and rode it to Bobet as he stood beside the road. Some even that there were no broken spokes and that Bobet had a simple flat tire. But whatever the truth, Bobet's inconvenience gave Schaer sudden fresh energy and he took a minute's lead.

Bobet was offended. This man who'd clung to his wheel was now profiting from misfortune to win an undeserved world championship. In the words of a French newsreel commentator, Bobet got back to Schaer "with a superhuman effort." And then, one last time over the Balhaüsen hill, he dismissed his rival.

Bobet crossed the line, drawn and ghostly, with 12 seconds' lead and a slight wave of his right hand. He had won the Tour and the world championship in the same year, the first Frenchman to do so since Georges Speicher in 1933. "You can't imagine how much I suffered to get back to Schaer after my wheel went," he said in his high-pitched voice. "I thought I'd lost a title that I deserved. Not for anything in the world would I relive that chase."

He was never popular, Bobet. Raphaël Géminiani said of him: "He lacked humility. But that was Bobet. He genuinely thought that after him there'd be no more cycling in France." Orson Welles came to encourage him once. "You have the good fortune to shake the hand of Louison Bobet," Bobet told him.

As well as other oddities, Bobet was superstitious about the number 41. He asked before each race who was wearing it. It had been in 1941 that he won his first race, in the 41st infantry regiment that he did his army service, and at 41 rue de la Roublot in Fontenay-sous-Bois that he lived.

He retired in August 1962 and opened a center for thalassotherapy, treatment by seawater, at Quiberon. He died after a long illness when he was 58 and lies now in the graveyard at St-Méen-le-Grand, in Brittany, under a simple slab of polished marble engraved "Louison Bobet 1925–1983." The Louison Bobet museum there displays the rainbow jersey he won that day in 1954.

1954
Brits on a roll

A decade would pass before Britain had another track championship as good as 1954 at Cologne. Reg Harris won the professional sprint and a south London glassblower called Cyril Peacock the amateur race, beating John Tressider of Australia and Roger Gaignard of France. Pete Brotherton came second and Norman Sheil third in the amateur pursuit, and Joe Bunker was third in the professional motor-pace.

Harris and Peacock were the last British sprint winners before Chris Hoy in 2008. They had their pictures on Player's cigarette cards in 1957. By then, Peacock had joined Harris as a professional for Raleigh.

Harris rode his bike in the real world but lived the rest in fantasy. That extended to buying his way to his comeback national championship, when he bribed Trevor Bull to let him win at the age of 54. Bull, a slow-speaking Midlander who died in 2009, was a lot more open about it than Harris. He'd asked his sponsor for a bonus if he won, he said, and when he was refused he happily took even more from Harris. The picture of the two approaching the line was as dramatic as they come but Harris' chain was taut and Bull's wasn't.

His biographer, Robert Dineen, said: "Perhaps such deception came easily to Harris because he had so often tinkered with the truth: from the implausible reason for the failed mechanic's apprenticeship, to the myriad exaggerated injuries, to the desperate need to explain away any defeat. He changed his accent, fudged his background and was unnecessarily formal with his speech."

Les Woodland

1956
First indoor world championship

It was back in 1888 that Nick Kaufman, who's credited with inventing cycle-ball, held the first artistic cycling championship. Details of the event are hazy and some accounts say he was more interested in promoting a brand of bicycles.

The UCI promoted the first championships for men in 1956, in Copenhagen, the first for women in Stuttgart in 1970. The sport is most popular in Germany, which has 10,000 licensed riders. The Swiss dominated the sport from 1956 to 1963, after which Germans won all but two championships until 2013.

Indoor cycling is similar to rhythmic gymnastics in that competitors, individually or in pairs, compete to music for five minutes.

1956
First cycle speedway championship

Cycle speedway is the pedal version of motorcycle speedway. Its origins are in races held on short circuits on partly cleared bomb sites in Britain, and especially London, during and after the second world war. There were 200 clubs in eastern London alone by 1950.

The rules were standardized in 1950 with the creation of a national body. A similar interest grew in the Netherlands, which was also heavily bombed, and a match between British and Dutch riders in the Earls Court exhibition hall in central London in 1950 was said to have been watched by 10,000. The sport declined as bomb sites were cleared but world championships are still held.

The first was in 1956 in Hilversum, the broadcasting capital of Holland. It was won by a Dutchman, Martin van der Brakel. The race has subsequently been held in England, Scotland, Australia, Poland and the USA, with British and Australian venues dominating. Riders ride oval-shaped circuits of around 80 meters on fixed-wheel bikes with upturned dropped handlebars. They previously used wide, V-shaped bars known as cowhorns.

Brett Aitken, who won the madison at the 2000 Olympics, started in the sport through cycle speedway.

Cycling's World Championships

1958
Hercules the colossus

Forli, Italy, forms a triangle with the gaudy coastal resort of Ravenna and the independent enclave of San Marino, up on its hill. Call a phone number in Forli and a man will come to open the Ercole Baldini museum. Not enough people want to see it to make it worth keeping open all the time.

Ercole is an old-fashioned name. It means Hercules and, sure enough, in 1958 Ercole stood astride the world. He was the stylish, smooth-pedaling outsider who won even though the romantic, and only the romantic, dreamed that Fausto Coppi could do it instead.

Baldini was no outsider. He won the Olympic road race and broke the world hour record in 1956, he won the Italian road championship in 1957 and 1958, and he won the 1958 Giro. He was an obvious pick for the 1958 world championship in Reims in northern France.

Nostalgia lived on, though, and the team included a drained Coppi, a shadow of his best. Baldini knew and respected him; he had pulled him round the Baracchi Trophy time trial in 1957, which was Coppi's last win and his first for two years. The world's manager, Alfredo Binda, was in the same position. He wasn't sure Coppi could even finish the race so, if sentiment insisted he was there, the others could benefit from his instructions if not his legs as the race went on. And his first advice was that small breaks had to have one Italian with them and that larger breaks needed two, riders whom Coppi would nominate.

The instructions worked well. Louison Bobet attacked with the big-chinned Dutchman, Gerrit Voorting. Bobet was past his best and although Voorting wore the yellow jersey in the Tours of 1956 and 1958, the danger didn't look that great. It ranked as a small break and so one Italian, Gastone Nencini, jumped in to join them. There was a long way to go. In time they'd die and then the real race could begin.

Coppi then told Baldini to ride up to them. He objected but Coppi insisted and Baldini used his hour-record speed to catch them in a couple of kilometers.

"Nencini asked me what I was doing," he told the journalist, Herbie Sykes. "I explained that I hadn't wanted to come across but that Coppi had insisted. Nencini shrugged his shoulders and didn't say anything. Maybe he thought Coppi was a cretin."

The break pressed on, Baldini driving it. Voorting flaked and faded. And then Nencini began to suffer. They'd ridden 165 kilometers off the front and there were 50 kilometers left. Nencini spoke fast Italian so that Bobet wouldn't understand. "I'm finished and so is Bobet", he said. "Attack him now." So Baldini attacked and held a two-minute lead to the line to win the world championship.

But rumors began to spread. The first reports praised Coppi, the old hero who could no longer win but had the wisdom to guide others. By contrast, Baldini was just a big strong lad who succeeded only with the master's magic. And then a darker story spread: that Coppi was jealous that Baldini, the new star, had begun to eat into his appearance money at track meetings, that it was better to send him on a suicide mission than have him win.

"It was a business decision," Baldini realized. "I don't mind that Fausto sent me, because it was logical for him. What bothers me is the fact that still, all these years on, journalists continue to misinterpret what happened and why. Coppi sent me because he wanted me to lose and he even admitted as much."

Well, in the words of a French assessment: "Ercole Baldini became a victim of his glory. He went from one excess to another and gave off an air of nonchalance. That doesn't mix with the life of a great cycling champion. Baldini should have been a *rouleur* like Coppi, a climber like Bartali, as resistant as Magni, but he was none of those. Satisfied with his early glory, he preferred the *dolce vita*."

He called it a day in November 1964 after coming second in the Baracchi time trial with Vittorio Adorni.

1958
The first women's championship

The male world world of cycling wasn't fast to accept championships for women. It took years of campaigning by a handful of countries to persuade the UCI to accept women.

The first champion was Elsy Jacobs of Luxembourg, in 1958. She won after 59 kilometers on the Gueux car circuit at Reims, France. The distance was typical for another 40 years.

The year before the championship, she moved to Paris "to live near- er where the races are." She trained under the direction of Raymond

Cycling's World Championships

Louviot, a former professional and later a prominent team manager.

The most dominant rider in the history of women's racing is Marianne Vos of Holland. By the start of 2015, she had won the road championship in 2006, 2012 and 2013, the cyclo-cross in 2006 and then every year from 2009 to 2014. She also won the track points championship in 2008 and the scratch in 2011.

Without her helmet on, she's rarely recognized even in Holland, she said. And sometimes not even when she gets mixed up with a group of men while training. They refuse to let her ride past them. But she insists. "And they ask 'Do you do races?' and I say 'Well, yeah, sometimes...' And they ask 'Well, have you won something?' I say 'Yeah, last year some races.' And they ask 'Are you Marianne Vos?' Then it's OK. And then they say 'Oh, yeaaah!' And then I may ride past."

Jeannie Longo, of France won the world road race in 1985, 1986, 1987 1989 and 1995, and the time trial in 1995, 1996, 1997 and 2001. She also won 31 national championships.

The championships of 1958 were the first under the influence of eastern European countries and the introduction of a road race, track sprint and pursuit for women and the reintroduction of motor-paced racing for men was due to greater influence from the Soviet bloc on the previously western-dominated UCI.

The introductions weren't without consequence. The Soviet Union won the women's sprint—Galina Ermolaeva—and pursuit—Ludmilla Kotchetova.

1959
The triumph of a rhubarb farmer

The three things that every British enthusiast knew of Beryl Burton were: first, that she won everything; second, that she had a no-nonsense Yorkshire accent; and third, that she worked on a rhubarb farm. To that you could add that she rode everywhere on her bike because she liked it and she never learned to drive, and that she knitted between championship heats.

Her daughter, Denise, said: "She'd be knitting away like mad pre-race or in between races because it helped her keep her concentration."

The ground had been set for her at the first world championships, in Paris in 1958. Ludmilla Kotchetova of the Soviet Union won the pursuit but Britons, Stella Ball and Kay Ray, came second and third. And then Burton took over. In 1959, at Rocourt in Liège, she reached the final to face Elsy Jacobs of Luxembourg. Jacobs had won the first women's road championship, the previous summer. She was a formidable opponent not just because of that but because later that year she set a world record for the hour at 41.35 kilometers. But Burton won, with Kotchetova third.

She won the pursuit championship in 1959 and 1960, then again in 1962, 1963 and 1966. She came second in 1961, 1964 and 1968 and third in 1967, 1971 and 1973. She also won the road race in 1960 and 1967. Her club-mate, Malcolm Cowgill, said: "We always talk: what would Beryl have done today with the track at Manchester, all the equipment and support? The eastern Europeans were souped up to the eyeballs. How many gold medals did that cost her? Back then, the women's world road race was run over ridiculous distances like 25 miles. If it had been what it is now—say 80 miles—she'd have been the last one standing. It'd be tailor-made for her."

Burton won the British time trial all-rounder championship (25, 50 and 100 miles) for 25 consecutive years, and won 72 national time trial championships. She died on her bike, from a heart attack, while delivering invitations to her 59th birthday party.

1962
Stab in the back

"There's an irony," said Jean Bobet, the brother of Louison and now a historian of the sport, "that the championships were held in a town called Salo. Whereas, in French, *salaud* means something else."

Precisely, it's a strong way of calling someone a bastard. Which is how many remember Jean Stablinski after those championships, although the truth will never be known.

Shay Elliott, the Irishman who many thought deserved to win and who also happened to be Stablinski's brother-in-law, made little secret of being for sale. He earned more, he said, from helping others and from selling races. And that's what many thought had happened at Salo. André Darrigade remembered: "They were great friends. They used to train together, and I think Stablinski was godfather to Shay's son. They prepared really well for the championship, riding behind a Derny and so on, and Shay could have been world champion that day."

So why wasn't he?

Bobet said: "It was an affair that people didn't speak about openly. It was a mysterious business and Shay was the victim once again."

For all that Elliott sold races, he needed a world championship, or any big win. Like all riders from outside the Continent, he was the victim of a rule that teams must take most of their riders from the country in which they were registered. There were no teams in Ireland and so Elliott sought work with the French, in this case with the St-Raphaël team for which Stablinski also rode. It was a buyer's market and Elliott would always be paid less than a French rider of the same ability.

So, he had a choice: he could win the championship himself and improve his value, or he could help Stablinski and pocket a bonus and keep his place with St-Raphaël. Legend says that he chose the second, for the money, for his employer and for his friendship. But it may not have been like that, which is why Bobet spoke of Elliott's being "a victim."

Elliott knew he was the fittest of the four in the break. "But I was out-numbered three to one. I could have been twice as fit as I was but just through force of numbers, I would have been beaten." He was there with Stablinski, Rolf Wolfsohl and Jos Hoevenaars. And, he said of Stablinski: "He wouldn't normally have had the Belgian and the German riding for him. But a little bit of coaxing on his behalf and he got them across to his side of the fence."

Seeing what was happening, Elliott attacked by himself. The other three chased immediately. But when Stablinski counter-attacked, nobody chased. He gained 30 seconds with 20 kilometers left and then a minute at the top of the Tormini climb. Stablinski won and Elliott was second at 1 minute 22 seconds.

Elliott owned up to many things and, when money was tight, he sold the secrets of the peloton to a Sunday paper in Britain, which led to his being ostracized by other riders. But he never said that he had sold the world championship to Stablinski. He was the fittest, he needed the race more than the Frenchman, and he considered himself stabbed in the back by his best friend. And yet many years later, he told *Cycling*: "I'm not supposed to say that I helped Jean, but he's the best friend I've got in cycling and godfather to my son, Pascal. So I couldn't very well go after him, could I?"

It's all a mystery. Maybe Stablinski felt guilty. Or maybe he was sending the elevator back, as the French put it. Whatever the reason, he slowed a break in the following year's Tour de France to let Elliott take Ireland's first yellow jersey. That would have helped his bargaining position and pushed up his fees in street races. But what happened at Salo will be forever a puzzle. All we know is that nothing went right after that. His marriage to Stablinski's sister began to fail, the hotel that he owned cost him his money, and he returned to Dublin in 1967. He tried racing with the Sunday professionals in Britain but gave up and in May 1971, two weeks after the death of his father, he shot himself dead.

The amateur race was won by a local rider, Renato Boncioni, and Belgium took all three medals in the women's race, with Marie-Rose Gaillard, Yvonne Reynders and Marie-Thérèse Naessens.

1962
The first team time trial championship

The first 100-kilometer time trial championship for teams of four riders was over two laps of 56 kilometers in Brescia. Italy beat a Danish team that included Ole Ritter, later the world hour record holder.

The championship was held every year until 1972, after which it was dropped in Olympic years. It was last held for national teams in Agrigento, Italy, in 1994. It came back in 2012 in Valkenburg, Holland, but for trade teams. It was then that the UCI began a team time trial for women as well.

1963
The hand of Benoni

The day a soccer player called Diego Maradona extended the concept of the game to include pushing the ball across the line with his hand, he said he had kept Argentina in the World Cup "with the head of Maradona and the hand of God." That was 1986. A couple of decades earlier, Benoni Beheyt must have felt the same way. Because he won the world road championship at Renaix by "fending off" his leader, the local hope and the race favorite, Rik van Looy. It seemed so improbable that even the president of the Belgian federation, Arnold Standaert, ran to the finish line to ask how it had happened.

If you have ever thought you understand Belgian cycling, it can only be because it was badly explained. Not only was there fighting was going on in the team, there were plenty of individual grudges outside it. Van Looy's influence extended to who won races and who got to race where. He was not widely liked. Jan Janssen, the Dutch world champion and Tour winner, said he admired him as a rider "but, as a man, *niks*." That unpopularity was worsened by his habit of surrounding himself with the heavies of his Red Guard, the numerous teams he led which wore red jerseys, who neutralized races until their master could attack or sprint.

Van Looy demanded the same devotion in world championships but he never got it. Like most nations, Belgium met before the race to decide allegiances. Deals are done between riders and sponsors to decide whether to ride for an individual, for Belgium or for themselves. Half the team may be riding for one leader, the other half for someone else. Not to mention those who saw their allegiance not to Belgium but to any foreigner who rode the rest of the year in the same trade team. Whatever the deal, money was to change hands, usually on the promise of bonuses afterward. Van Looy offered $1,500 to anyone prepared to help if he won.

Beheyt was to ride for van Looy. He had no objection because he didn't see himself as a winner and because van Looy would cough up if, as was likely, he won before a home crowd. But others were far less happy. Yes, they'd take part but they weren't going to help van Looy. Just the opposite.

Why? Because van Looy had won Milan–San Remo in 1958 thanks to the sweat of his teammates and then, according to Gilbert Desmet, not paid them. More than that, said Desmet, he had himself been about to win the Tour of Flanders and then Paris–Roubaix when van Looy prevented it. It's less clear where Beheyt stood but when the time came at Renaix that van Looy called for his riders to get him to the front for a mass sprint, Beheyt said he was too tired to help and Desmet, given the job of leading out van Looy in the sprint, contrived to do it far too soon, leaving van Looy by himself and struggling to keep up his speed.

Beheyt could see van Looy weakening on his high gear and pushed up alongside him so that, if his boss didn't win, at least it would be another Belgian. He said van Looy was struggling so much on a big gear that he had start riding off at an angle. That's why he had reached out, to prevent a crash.

The pictures show his hand but it's hard to see if his fingers have grabbed the jersey or are simply pushing. Van Looy protested and wanted Beheyt disqualified. But the judges told him to keep quiet; they'd have disqualified for him for hindering Beheyt if he'd crossed the line first.

Van Looy never forgot. He made Beheyt's life such a misery, while remaining polite in public and profiting from revenge matches around the country, that the world champion abandoned racing at 25.

1965
Simpson's surprise

Sometimes you can't help being surprised at how races turn out. Even the most fervent of British supporters in 1965 admitted to a tingling doubt when their man, Tom Simpson, won in a two-up sprint with Rudi Altig of Germany. Why? Because Simpson was a brave but hollow-chested guy too light to be a serious road sprinter. Certainly not up against the hefty Altig, who had honed his talent on the track and still spent his winters on the fast boards of the six-day circuit. Eyebrows rose, although both men insisted it had been a fair fight.

The road races were at Lasarte, outside San Sebastian, just round from where France and Spain join beside the Atlantic. Simpson shared the driving from his home in Belgium with an Australian, Nev Veale, who'd won his national road championship in 1961 and was trying to make a living in Europe. The two reached Lasarte two or three days before the championship. Simpson was happy enough to be there but he didn't rate his chances high enough to be worth paying for a soigneur.

That day of the championship, the rain in Spain fell on the plain as well as the handsome. The race went on for six and a half hours. Simpson had the agreement of other British riders to help him. Some were full-timers on the continent and others weekend professionals back home. Two of the full-timers, Alan Ramsbottom and Vin Denson, helped get Simpson up to a break. Altig was one of those who

Cycling's World Championships

came with them and, after various changes, it was he who was alone with Simpson on the climb outside Hernani.

The two knew each other from the classics and the Tour de France and also because they had ridden as a team in the Baracchi time trial in Italy. They got on well because and shared a sense of humor.

Simpson said in his autobiography: "I cannot explain it, call it intuition or what you like, but I could not accept that Altig could beat me. Going round the back of the circuit we came to a gentleman's agreement. Both of us had worked hard in our little break and therefore we each deserved an equal chance of victory. We agreed to separate when we reached the one-kilometer-to-go board and ride in side by side. Altig was quite happy about this for I am sure he thought he could put it across me."

Simpson led on the final descent and on through spectators on the streets of Lasarte. He started to sprint way well before the line and kept going, expecting Altig to come by. "And suddenly, when I was ten yards from the line, it dawned on me. 'He hasn't! He hasn't made it! It's Mine!'"

He pulled up, went to the podium in his Peugeot jersey rather than the blue and red of Britain—a hint to his team to keep him employed, and for which he was fined—and when he finally saw his bike again he saw the back tire was worn over a stretch a little less long than his little finger. Another few minutes' riding and it would have burst.

He left Spain quickly, driving back across the border, to Biarritz, to fly to Paris for a race the next day. He left behind not only his gold medal but his shorts and champion's jersey. He borrowed shorts from Raymond Poulidor and shoes and socks from Jan Janssen.

Simpson always insisted that there was no deal, financial or otherwise, that he should win. Altig says the same thing. And that's the end of the story. But at least some of Simpson's teammates that day say he cheated the dope control with urine from a British cycling official, now dead. Two years later, Simpson was himself dead on Mont Ventoux, in the Tour de France, with drugs a factor in his collapse.

Chapter 6: 1966 – 1975

Merckx and the outsiders, an era of surprise winners

1966
The day of the third thief

The French call him the third thief, the villain who watches the other two bicker over the bounty and then makes off with it himself. That was Rudi Altig on his home ground of the Nürburgring.

At the time, the two most prominent riders in the world were French. They were rivals who for a long time wouldn't even speak to each other. Despite that, the selectors in Paris put Jacques Anquetil and Raymond Poulidor in world championship teams even though neither of them won. There were occasional medals but the war between them ruled out anything better. The coldly commercial Anquetil saw no benefit in being world champion but realized that his own earnings would be cut if Poulidor won. The outcome was obvious.

Anquetil and Poulidor were both in the winning break in 1966. They'd dropped Altig, and those who couldn't read tarot cards thought all was going well.

But Anquetil was the man who could drop nobody but whom nobody could drop. So he and Poulidor went slowly enough that Altig could come back up to them, bringing a third Frenchman, Lucien Aimar, with him. The question now was whether Aimar was just guarding Altig to limits his chances, or if he was working with him to catch the break.

Why is that a question? Because three Frenchmen would outnumber a single German, of course, but also because Aimar and Anquetil were in the same trade team, Ford-France. He had an allegiance to France but his salary meant that loyalty was more to Anquetil than to Poulidor, whom anyway he didn't like. But Altig was no fool and he started his sprint 300 meters out to give all three Frenchmen time to study each other and become confused. Which is what they did. Altig beat first Anquetil and then Poulidor, all in the same time.

The amateur race was won by the glassy-eyed Dutchman, Eef Dolman—who later said he had taken drugs throughout his career—ahead of the Briton, Les West.

The amateur sprint brought the first gold medal for Daniel Morelon, of France. He won again in 1967, every year from 1969 to 1973, then again in 1975. He won a record nine amateur world championships between 1966 and 1975 as well as three Olympic gold medals.

1967
New kid on the block

If you're ever in a pub quiz which asks which riders have won both the amateur and professional road championships, the answer is, in order, Jean Aerts, Hans Knecht and Eddy Merckx. And if you're also asked who was the youngest ever winner of the pro race, here's a hint: it wasn't Merckx and it wasn't Lance Armstrong.

Merckx won the amateur race at Sallanches in 1964 and then the pro race at Heerlen, in Holland, in 1967. Which was a sort of theatrical unveiling because Merckx until then had raced largely in Belgium.

Merckx was only 19 when he turned professional and started and then dropped out of the Flèche Wallonne. He won nine races but his season ended unhappily because he was riding in the red-shirted Solo team led by Rik van Looy and paid for by a margarine company. Solo's tactics were simple: van Looy had to win. Taking on a 19-year-old with good legs and teenage awkwardness soon proved an unhappy idea.

Within the year, Merckx had signed for the French team, Peugeot, making the most of his bilingual background. That put him in competition for top place with Tom Simpson, which indirectly led to Simpson's death, but the settled atmosphere and the extra year did him good and he won Milan–San Remo.

The circuit at Heerlen wasn't demanding, so Merckx rode 18 races in 22 days as preparation, relying on the speed of Belgian street races to give him the edge. And, unusually for a favorite, he went with the first break, which happened after only five kilometers. And, unusually again, the break stayed away.

In it were Gianni Motta, who'd won the Giro the previous year; Ramón Sáez of Spain; the Dutchman Jos van der Vleuten—who finished fifth but was caught in a drugs test and disqualified; and a tall and toothy weekend professional from Britain. For Bob Addy, who was sponsored by a bike shop near the Thames and worked during the week as a refrigerator salesmen, it was the highlight of his career; for Merckx, in his memoirs, he was just "an English rider who never came to the front."

Addy faded at half distance and van der Vleuten had little interest in propelling the quintet because his leader, Jan Janssen, was trying to get up to the break to join them. Janssen had won the pro title the day after Merckx had won the amateur race at Sallanches. Merckx wasn't inclined to let him succeed again but, all the same, Janssen reached the leaders in a single lap.

Van der Vleuten led out the sprint for Janssen but Merckx passed him with Janssen on his left and Sáez to the other side. And he stayed a wheel ahead of Janssen to become the second youngest world pro road champion ever. He was 22, two years older than the 1934 champion, Karel Kaers.

Legend says that Armstrong was the youngest winner, at 21, in Oslo in 1993. But it ain't necessarily so.

1967
And I'll be the last British champion

The day Graham Webb won the amateur road championship in Holland, he half-heartedly raised one hand as he crossed the line because he was thinking: "Oh no, what if someone's away? What a fool I'll look." Because of his gangly, slow-talking way, and a whining Birmingham accent, a British official said he was so thick that he didn't even know he'd won.

"That was going a bit far," Webb said drily.

He won the race alone after riding flat out through the last corner and tilting his bike so far he couldn't be sure it would cling to the floor.

"And there were journalists all asking me questions and one of them said it was the first time for 45 years that a British rider had won the world championship. It was a guy called Dave Marsh, who won it when it was a time trial and it was held in England. And I remember saying 'And they'll have to wait another 45 years before another British rider wins.' And I meant it. I knew what talent I had and what I had to do. It sounds big-headed to say it but it was true."

He was despairing at the British fixation on time trialing and the population's island mentality. And it turned out to be literally true because the UCI scrapped the amateur category before another British man won.

"There was no lead car to show we were at the front of the race, just a load of photographers' motorbikes. I'd already planned that I'd go a mile from the finish. I just needed a yard. It may sound big-headed but I knew that if I could get a yard then they wouldn't catch me. When you stand there on the podium, it doesn't sink in what you've done. But then I saw my mum up on the podium there with me. I didn't even know she was in Holland.

"I've still got the gold medal and I show it to my grandchildren sometimes. But I haven't got that rainbow jersey any more. I turned pro after the championships but legend says that Merckx was the youngest winner except for only by 21-year-old Armstrong in Oslo in 1993—it's a very long story—things went dreadfully wrong. I used to have a bar in Ghent and I hung the jersey on the wall. But it got filthy because of the cigarette smoke and customers would make remarks about it and, because I was really depressed about how things had turned out, one day I took it off the wall and threw it into the stove.

"It's sentimental but I was hoping my grandson would be the first British rider after me to win the men's world road race. But he's stopped racing."

1969
In Harm's way

An outsider beat a rider who was only a little less an outsider to win the pro championship in 1969—and all because the world was set on stopping the favorite.

Harmin Ottenbros, known as Harm, made the Dutch team for Zolder at the last moment only because its leader, Jan Janssen, had

Cycling's World Championships

fallen ill and there was room for someone at the bottom. Ottenbros was available and so he went, a man who had ridden little other than local criteriums but who'd be good cannon-fodder for the better riders. He'd be the man to bring them bottles and chase into the wind. Instead of that, he won that August 10 and it ruined his life. He ended up abandoning cycling and living in a squat.

It happened because he was the collateral damage in a civil war in Belgian and even world cycling. Eddy Merckx was winning more and more and not only leaving almost nothing to others who also depended on cycling for their lives, but disturbing the *amour propre* of older stars such as Rik van Looy. Not only most of the bunch but half the Belgian team were so insistent that he shouldn't win that an hour before the end he picked a quiet part of the course and got off his bike and abandoned.

That left a vacuum. Deprived of their target, nobody knew what to do. That Merckx would just ride off to his hotel was something they'd never considered.

L'Équipe reported: "This world championship, just as we'd forecast, was held to ransom right from the start by the formula of national teams, by disagreements among the Belgians, and by the order of battle, which was to stop Eddy Merckx winning. For him, the best of all in terms of absolute talent, the problem looked insoluble. And it was. So the winner of the Tour de France, crushed by numbers, paralyzed by the hunting-wolves of the peloton left the race on the last lap so that his name never even figured in the results."

The bunch had so little plan that at the bell it let the break get to two minutes. And even that was blocked. Neither of the two biggest riders could attack. If Roger De Vlaeminck tried, the Dutch sprinter Gerben Karstens would go with him and beat him at the end. But Karstens couldn't attack without tiring himself and spoiling his sprint or, worse, having De Vlaeminck power past him. So they just watched each other.

Since no one else would do anything, Ottenbros and a Belgian, Julien Stevens, rode away with four kilometers to go. Now De Vlaeminck and Karstens had not just their original problem but the ethical snag that neither could chase his own teammate. Ottenbros and Stevens went to a straight sprint and Ottenbros won on the inside by centimeters.

"The nearer the finish line came," he said years later, "the more I had to tell myself I was just in a kermesse, although with a few more spectators than usual. I had to forget that I was riding for a world title because, if I'd realized that, I'd never have won."

Few were impressed. "The race needed a winner," sneered Pierre Chany, "and it was Ottenbros: Ottenbros, who finished the Tour de France in 78th place, three hours behind the yellow jersey."

The world of cycling turned on Ottenbros, the scapegoat for their own conscience, their pettiness. They stopped him winning even criteriums. Often he was lucky to get even start money. They jeered at his weakness on hills and called him "The Eagle of Hogerheide," an ironic reference to the flatness of south-west Holland. He earned no more as world champion—€2,500—than he had as an unknown.

Life just got worse. He broke his wrist in the Tour of Flanders and could neither ride in his rainbow jersey nor defend his title. Then his team folded. "I wasn't in the slightest bit sorry when my year as world champion was over and I didn't have to wear that jersey any more. I could just go back to being the unknown rider in village criteriums. I was never happy again," he said.

He considered suicide. His marriage broke up and he lost touch with his three children. Homeless now, he slept on the floor with the dropouts who had become his world.

Ottenbros lives now in a housing estate—a project, as they'd say in America—south of Rotterdam. Some days he glues tiles to walls and floors, other days he fits carpets. He works with mentally handicapped children in his spare time. His rainbow jersey and medal are in a closet but it's years since he looked at them.

"If I could live my life all over again," he says sadly, "I'd miss out the cycling bit."

1970
War without the shooting

George Orwell said that: that sport was war without shooting. And it became the policy of eastern European countries as the 1960s began, inspired by the admiration of the west for Emil Zátopek in athletics after world war two. Sport could show the superiority of the communist pattern, socially, and it could keep the west in place, psychologically.

Cycling's World Championships

And it could do that most effectively by concentrating on events least affected by chance.

There was no point at which you could say that eastern domination started. It was a gradual process. The Soviet Union won the team pursuit in 1963, 1964 and 1965 and the sprint in 1965. Communist nations, which had no professional sport, favored the Olympics. From the 1960s, eastern influence on the UCI extended enough to bring into world championships events that already existed at the Olympics: the men's team pursuit, 1,000-meter time trial, 100-kilometer team time trial and the tandem sprint. At the same time, cycling split into separate bodies for professionals and amateurs, which gave the communist bloc influence where it wanted.

From 1970 to 1979 the Soviet Union won the women's sprint seven times and the women's pursuit six times. East German men won fifteen gold medals on the road and track, Czechs won the tandem sprint four times and the Soviet Union won the team time trial four times.

The men's sprint title was won twice by the Czech, Anton Tkáč (1974 and 1978), by Hans-Jurgen Geschke of East Germany in 1977 and by Lutz Hesslich in 1979. From 1980 to 1987, East Germany and the Soviet Union each won seventeen gold medals and the far smaller Czechoslovakia seven. After that, of course, the communist experiment ended and, with it, the sports schools and laboratories which had helped produce that domination.

But...context is needed. While it's clear that the east dominated the west in amateur racing, there were two important considerations. The first was that amateur racing for many in the west was only a step to becoming a professional, whereas in the east amateur racing was all there was. The second was that while few westerners fitted the definition of amateurism the British imposed on the world in the 1800s, probably none of the eastern riders did. They were gathered into sports schools and given treatment and incentives that the rest of the population rarely saw, so that in practice they were as professional as the professionals.

But at least it never came to a real war.

Les Woodland

1972
Basso profundo

People who care about these things still get worked up about Marino Basso. Did he somehow steal the world championship from Franco Bitossi? To anyone not Italian, it's hard to see what the fuss is about. But there are many in the peninsula who won't let the dust settle.

The place is Gap, in France, and the race is 270 kilometers long with enough of a hill to send the weakest out the back. Basso had known from the day he saw a map of the circuit that he had every chance of being world champion. He'd have the legs from the Tour de France, and the kilometer-long finishing straight that climbed gently to the line was just what he needed. He confirmed it with a training ride round two laps and then set it as his plan for August.

Around two thirds of the race had passed when Basso got clear with almost everyone who mattered. Eddy Merckx was there and so was Felice Gimondi, and Bitossi and Roger De Vlaeminck and Cyrille Guimard, Jan Janssen, Frans Verbeeck, Raymond Poulidor and more. The move of the race had happened.

Half a dozen were left with three laps to go. Merckx didn't want that many and began attacking. It worked and it didn't work and Basso could see why.

"His weak point was that he always wanted to drop everybody, and so if you sat on his wheel, he would drive himself into the ground to get rid of you. When he saw you could stay with him, he cracked a little. I remember I even said 'I'm still here', at one point, playing a psychological game."

When Merckx couldn't do it, some of the others caught up again. Guimard tried his chance at the foot of the climb and Basso shouted for Bitossi to go after him. The problem now for Bitossi was that he was leading a world championship but he had one of the peloton's sharpest sprinters with him. So he attacked him and opened a gap.

Basso had shouted for Bitossi to chase Guimard because Bitossi was the weaker sprinter and therefore better used as a domestique. But now Basso realized he had blundered. Whatever the agreement had been in the Italian team, he actually wanted to win the race himself. He didn't want Bitossi storming along to the finish alone.

Cycling's World Championships

Bitossi himself remembered: "With three or four kilometers to go, Guimard took off and I followed him. Guimard was dangerous, being very fast. He expected my collaboration but I just drafted him to avoid wasting energy. I was hoping he could take me to the line. When he saw I wasn't working with him, he slowed down and the rest of the group reached us. I was fresh because I'd been drafting Guimard, so I took off. I thought 'Merckx is a friend and he's not going to chase me, Dancelli and Basso are Italian and therefore they're not going to try catching me either.'"

But that was to misjudge Basso…

"Seeing the world title slipping away, I knew I had to do something. I wanted to beat Bitossi but I couldn't chase him myself, otherwise they would have killed me back in Italy. I shouted at Merckx and Gimondi to do something but they knew I was going mad and let me suffer. I couldn't move because the television motorbike was filming us. But fortunately they had to leave us and go to the finish because we were getting close to the line.

"Still determined to win, as soon as they moved away I went on the front and drove hard for 600 meters through the center of Gap."

Bitossi again: "When I took off, nobody followed me and I immediately gained several meters. I thought I was going to be the world champion. And then there was a little climb. And that's where I made my mistake. Well, my teammates didn't do much to protect me…"

Basso: "When the others saw me working, they started as well, and we all started to believe we could still catch Bitossi and fight it out for the world title. Guimard did a long pull; Zoetemelk did a turn to help him and then Merckx went through."

Bitossi: "At the beginning of the climb, I changed to a lower gear. But then I had the feeling that it was too low. The line was there. It seemed I could almost touch it. But it never arrived, so I changed to a higher gear and that was my mistake. After 100 meters, my legs got stuck."

Basso: "When we got to the finish straight, I looked up and I could see Bitossi still had a 200-meter lead. There were only 600 meters to go and I could see he was dying."

Bitossi: "That day was windy. The wind was in my face and coming from the right. While riding that last kilometer I was protected by the people on the right side of the road. But when I realized I was getting stuck, I tried to see where the other riders were. I noticed they were really speeding up. I thought there was somebody trying to take off and catch me. But they were hidden by the two commissaires' cars and to see them I had to move in the middle of the road, where it was very windy. This slowed me down even more."

Basso: "I knew I could still win if I did two sprints: one to catch him and one to jump past and win. I wanted the rainbow jersey and I told myself I had to go at 250 meters from the line. I knew I might lead out the others but all I was thinking about was winning."

Bitossi: "He passed me with six or seven meters to go. I knew they were very close to me, but I was just pedaling in the wind and watching the line, hoping they wouldn't pass me. Now I laugh about that but when it happened it was hard to accept. I had been riding well all the day, trying to save my energy. I didn't want to make the same mistake I made the year before [1971 championship in Switzerland], when I had been in a break for 200 kilometers and then Merckx won. So that day I had been riding very carefully. It would have been my masterpiece, so I like calling it my Unfinished Masterpiece."

It was Merckx rather than Basso who caught Bitossi, because he'd jumped just a moment before Basso got round to it. But that hardly mattered because, without Basso, Merckx wouldn't have been there anyway. Basso may now pull Merckx's leg by saying he gave away the championship but that, perhaps, is to pass on the blame.

However Basso saw it then or later, nobody in Gap was deluded. Bitossi accused Basso of stabbing him in the back; Basso retaliated that he'd done no more than anyone else would have done and that, anyway, Bitossi had gone off on his own account even though he knew Basso was the stronger finisher.

The more they argued, the more each of them thought he was in the right. And the fans, those of them who care, are still just as divided.

1973
When stars fall out

Things ended well for Marino Basso in 1972 but they didn't start well in 1973. He started the world championship at Montjuich, near Barcelona, by flattening a policeman. The copper had been trying to stop him getting into an area he considered closed and Basso, who was there to defend the title he'd won the previous year, took a swing at him. He started the race convinced that he'd finish the day in jail. Not the best way to begin your day.

The local man was Luis Ocaña, whose ambition to aggravate Merckx was so pronounced that he named his dog Merckx for the pleasure of giving it orders and seeing it sit at his feet. Ocaña was there when the race produced its first significant break, around mid-distance. There, too, were Merckx, Felice Gimondi and a 21-year-old Belgian with big thighs, a flexible face and a devastating sprint: Freddy Maertens.

Maertens had been billed as the next Merckx even before he turned professional. His lack of respect when he did turn professional made him enemies within cycling generally and Belgian cycling in particular.

Merckx feigned an attack in the hope that others would take over and rid him of the menace within his own camp. Maertens asked him not to. "I'm cramping up," he told him too quietly for the others to hear. "If you don't attack, I'll lead you out in the sprint." According to Maertens, Merckx said: "I don't believe you." And then he attacked.

Maertens remembered: "There was no cooperation between Gimondi and Ocaña. As Merckx escaped, I was thinking that if I went as well, Ocaña wouldn't close the gap for Gimondi and it would have been just as unlikely that Gimondi would follow Merckx since they were both riding on Campagnolo equipment."

Maertens insists that Campagnolo, for years the traditional supplier of chainsets and pedals and gears, had offered bonuses to prevent anyone using the newly arrived Shimano, such as Maertens, from winning. Shimano, too, must have offered a bonus because Maertens let slip that he'd have been "a millionaire in a single day" had he won, although without saying in which currency.

"My plan worked and during the climb of Montjuich itself, I managed to get up to Merckx on my own and took over immediately. But to my absolute astonishment, he refused to share the lead. He just allowed Gimondi and Ocaña to come back up to us."

Maertens said again that he'd lead the sprint. There'd be no faster lead-out man.

Les Woodland

Merckx's version: "We got to the top of the last hill and Maertens took over, just as he said he would. He started the sprint with me on his wheel and Gimondi third, Ocaña behind him. We got to 200 meters from the line, when I wanted to sprint, but my legs wouldn't respond. I was in a black hole. My nerves gave out without warning. I saw Gimondi and Ocaña go past and the Italian jumped Maertens on the line."

Maertens' version was that Gimondi pushed him into the barriers. The two didn't speak for ages.

The Italians rejoiced, hugging and carrying Gimondi, while the Belgian camp had all the joy of an undertakers' convention. Merckx was supposed to win and, if he didn't, well, Maertens was supposed to outsprint everyone. But neither had happened.

Maertens wrote: "If Merckx and I had pooled our strength after he broke away earlier, we would easily have been able to stay out of reach. Afterward, some people said I was wrong to chase up to him. But why shouldn't I have done? I didn't do anything wrong. I didn't bring the other two up to him on my wheel. Just the opposite, in fact."

Ocaña, who realized now that he'd probably lost all hope of ever winning a world championship, looked as upset as he was puzzled. "I never thought Merckx would crack," he said, "but as soon as I saw it happen, I went after Gimondi. But I was too late. Another 20 meters and I could have been champion of the world", adding: "But better Gimondi than the other one", avoiding mentioning Merckx by name again.

The cold war between Merckx and Maertens lasted another decade, Merckx believing Maertens had duped him, Maertens offended at what he saw as Merckx's lack of gratitude. The whole team turned against him in the El Rancho hotel after the race: apart from any question of allegiance or national pride, they accused Maertens of costing them their bonus. Merckx stayed in his room, sulking, and only Herman van Springel and Rik van Linden could persuade him to leave.

"Maybe I was too fast for him," Maertens said years afterward. "I went full speed and Eddy was three or four lengths off my wheel. A sprinter isn't always a good lead-out man. We never spoke about money. At that time I would have been very happy to have been second after Merckx on the podium. Maybe Eddy didn't believe my words."

Cycling's World Championships

Ten years passed in which Merckx and Maertens never rode in the same trade team, in which neither would allow the other to win, in which Belgian supporters drinking their day away by the roadside had shouting matches over which was the better rider. And then one day there was reconciliation. Merckx and Maertens were in the same hotel before a race in the Beaujolais region of France.

Maertens said: "At first, when I saw him going up to his room, I thought I would never see him again. And then he came down. I was smoking a cigarette and he asked me for one. He said to me: 'Freddy, we have to talk about Barcelona.' I said: 'I think so, too.' And then we spoke about it for three hours and we shook hands and everything was over."

They talked until five in the morning.

"Before, all the journalists talked about us being not friends; since the time we became friends, no journalists ask me how it is!"

Those troubles were over but there were many more for Maertens. His sponsor, Flandria, folded and he said he was paid for only half of 1978. He also wasn't paid the under-the-table money he and the sponsor had agreed would be passed so that he wouldn't pay tax on it. Maertens speaks of it as though it were a perfectly normal way of doing business in professional cycling. The tax people, though, were wise to things like that and they pursued Maertens not only for what he'd been paid but for the year in which Maertens said he hadn't been paid beyond the middle of the season.

The more Maertens contested the tax bills, the more he paid in lawyers' fees and the more the interest, and then the interest on the interest, built up. He lost his house and almost all he owned, although his wife, Carine, stuck by him. "She saved my life," Maertens agrees.

It took 30 years to pay off the debt, the last coin handed over in June 2010. In all, he paid 30 million Belgian francs, around $1 million, five times more than he'd have expected.

Martens refused to go to the funeral for Paul Claeys, Flandria's owner. "He was not a good guy. He promised and promised…"

By that time Maertens had discovered he was an alcoholic; he had, although there may be no connection, taken to drinking sugared champagne towards the end of the race ("Lomme Driessens handed it up and then finished the bottle himself"). He became a wine connoisseur with a cellar of wine known throughout the élite of Belgian cycling. And when everything turned upside down, he went to a meeting of Alcoholics Anonymous only to find his unmistakeable face made him anything but anonymous. He works now as curator and guide in the Tour of Flanders museum in Oudenaarde, where he refuses any drink offered in the bar.

Gimondi reckoned that Merckx simply couldn't accept that he'd been beaten. "When Maertens started to lead out the sprint," he said, "I could follow him without difficulty, and you know that I'm not the best rider to cope with changes of speed. If a rider like Eddy couldn't close the gap, the only reason could be that he didn't have the legs. On any other day, he'd have won the race on one leg. If Maertens had really wanted to win on his own account, he'd have put two car lengths into us."

And Marino Basso? He finished 27th. And he didn't go to jail.

1975
Hennie beats 10½ men

There's a picture you may have seen of the 1975 Tour de France. Bernard Thévenet has just stuck with Merckx and then reduced him to frustration. After a decade of Merckx monopoly, the moment seemed more striking then than it does now. Striking enough that a woman has drawn herself a large sign to stand by the roadside to taunt Merckx with its message: "The Bastille has fallen."

The sign is hardly accurate. Merckx was Belgian rather than French, of course. But the sentiment and emotion were strong enough that Merckx's defeat was likened to the one event that everyone knows of: the French Revolution.

Merckx is a proud man and one prone to seek revenge. After a spring in which he'd won Milan–San Remo, the Tour of Flanders, Liège–Bastogne–Liège and the Amstel Gold Race, being upended in the Tour wasn't to his liking. So he looked forward to the world championship because it was in his own country, at Yvoir on the edge of the Ardennes, and because it was on that very circuit that he'd won the national championship five years earlier. If he could win again, he'd be the first man to win four world road championships.

Cycling's World Championships

To help him, he'd have what one Belgian paper called "the greatest fighting army ever assembled," of which five riders were his own team-mates the rest of the year.

The Dutch were riding for Joop Zoetemelk, who was taunted all round the circuit by Belgians waving giant orange lollipops to suggest he did little more than suck Merckx's wheel. That the Dutch would all ride for Zoetemelk, they'd decided with their manager, the former world champion Jan Janssen, then still the only Dutchman to win the Tour de France. So when a break went on the first lap, Hennie Kuiper put himself in it to slow things down.

The betting was all on Merckx, but those who wagered lost their money because he tangled up with a spectator on the fourth lap and fell. That knocked the hope out of him and he told Roger De Vlaeminck that from then on he'd ride for him.

De Vlaeminck was in the final break, along with Kuiper, Lucien van Impe, Felice Gimondi, Gerrie Knetemann and others. Kuiper, the cruelest assessment said, could win a sprint only if he had two blocks' lead. So, with nothing to lose, he went off by himself with 24 kilometers left. The others chased, of course, but they lost the race by 150 meters. Disappointing for the also-rans but, as so often, there was something that neither the others in the break nor the crowd at the finish knew.

Before the race, Roger De Vlaeminck had interrupted a Belgian federation official speaking at a pre-race dinner about the 11 members of the Belgian team. No, he said: there were only 10½. It was a good and, you'd think, harmless joke. But Lucien van Impe, who was the butt of it, wasn't so tickled. And van Impe, who was no taller than a climber needed to be, seethed and then brooded.

At the finish, De Vlaeminck finished second despite his team's help. But perhaps not van Impe's. "He told me later that the remark had cost me his support and therefore, maybe, the world championship," De Vlaeminck said, half amused, half wondering at the truth of it. He thought he was certain of winning, but the truth was that he chased Kuiper too late because he just couldn't believe Merckx, his old enemy, didn't have a trick to pull.

"I missed my chance," De Vlaeminck said. The Belgian crowd thought so, too. They whistled.

Everybody else may have felt discontent, as well. David Saunders, of the *Daily Telegraph* in Britain, wrote: "The riders, managers, helpers and press who attended the 1975 world cycling championships in Belgium had every right to be critical. Poor planning, bad organization, lack of thought and consideration, utter incompetence and downright carelessness can all be justifiably leveled at the officials in charge. Add to that the awful state of the Rocourt track. Things did not improve for the road events. Perhaps justice was done in the end, though, as the great cycling nation of Belgium failed to earn a single gold medal during the championships."

1975
The triumph of Navajo Sue

"Those were the seventies, remember," Sue Novara says. "Having a lot of hair was important back then."

Sue Novara-Reber, as she is now, whirred into world sprinting at Monteroni, all lean legs and a mane of hair to her waist. She was just 19, a youthful novelty in the hitherto straight-faced world of women's racing. In America, her long hair gave her the nickname Navajo Sue.

She wanted originally to be a speed skater, not difficult in the cold winters of Flint, Michigan, but at 13 she turned to cycling. At 18, in 1975, it took a photo to decide she had come second in the world championship to Iva Zajikova of Czechoslovakia and so close was the finish that some records still list Novara as the winner.

Novara won again in 1980, at Besançon, and then handed the rainbow to Sheila Young in 1981 and Connie Paraskevin in 1982, 1983 and 1984.

"Back then it was just the start of possibilities for young girls in athletics in other areas but we didn't have that privilege," she remembered two decades later. "Maybe we just had to try harder just to be noticed, not just in sports generally but in cycling. Perhaps that's what made the difference. And there weren't all the intermediate steps: there was the national championship and there was the world championship and there was nothing else. We not only had to win but to win over and over just to get noticed."

She rode her last race in New York in 1984. She no longer rides a bike, "because Flint isn't bike-friendly." She spends her spare time in Swaziland, with children orphaned because of AIDS.

Cycling's World Championships

"Bike racing was good and I shall always know I was champion of the world because I have my medals and my jerseys in a cabinet here at home. I'm proud of that, sure, but what I'm doing in Africa means far more."

Chapter 7: 1976 – 1989

Back from the dead: Two great riders win, vanish, and come back to win again

1976
First human-powered championships

The UCI keeps a strict control of the bikes it allows in competition. It banned recumbent bicycles, in which the rider lies horizontally, in 1934. That was after three Frenchmen beat Oscar Egg's world hour record on one.

Despairing of rules they saw as pointlessly restrictive and which would never let cycling show what it could do, Dr. Chester Kyle, a professor of bio-mechanical engineering at California State University in Long Beach, formed the Human-Powered Vehicle Association in 1976. Its races and records allow any vehicle moved only by human power, although it groups different classes such as tricycles and tandems.

The 24-hour record set by Christian von Ascheberg in August 2010 is 1,219 kilometers. His 12-hour record is 665 kilometers. He died in 2013, after a heart attack while cycling.

1976
Maertens the majestic

Without someone to look after him, Freddy Maertens' wife said, he'd be like a bird waiting for a cat. The first dominant figure was his father, so controlling that he cut his son's race bike in half after seeing him do no more than talk to a girl. The second was the team manager, Lomme Driessens. When he had one or the other, he was close to unbeatable; with neither, he was a figure of fun.

In 1976 he had Driessens and he won the national championship, four classics, eight stages of the Tour de France, six of Paris–Nice and, over the season, 55 victories. Nobody has done better, especially when you remember that one of those wins was the world championship at Ostuni, Italy. And there he had a team obliged to ride for him because there was no sensible alternative. Merckx had started his decline and the fast course, without real problems, favored a sprinter.

"Even Merckx rode for me," Maertens remembered years later, still not sure he could believe it.

Francesco Moser thought he had the race settled before his home crowd when he broke clear with Joop Zoetemelk, a sturdy Tour rider but a weaker sprinter. That was to reckon without a united Belgian team, though, which put Maertens close enough that he could reach the leaders, with Moser's teammate, Tino Conti, on his wheel to make things difficult.

Moser then attacked going down the last hill, to get rid of Zoetemelk and, with luck, Maertens as well. The Belgian looked tired after the Tour de France, which Moser hadn't ridden, and then the round of criteriums he had ridden afterward. Maertens missed taking his turn a couple of times as the two tried to stay away from the chase but onlookers couldn't decide if he was bluffing and being lazy or if he really was no match for Moser's greater cruising speed.

In fact it was bluff: Maertens said that, sure, he'd been cooked but he had to exaggerate his tiredness to distract Moser. For close on a kilometer, Maertens refused to come by, while Moser looked repeatedly over his shoulder to see what was going on. The pace slowed with 500 meters to go and then it was Maertens who began looking back, because Conti and Zoetemelk were only 10 seconds behind and the main field less than 20 seconds behind them. Maertens said:

> He attacked twice, on both occasions after he'd taken shelter behind a Citröen with the television camera. When he did it a third time, I'd had enough.

"I'm not doing any more in front," I told him.

"I can see the chasers gaining on us," he said, trying to make me change my mind.

"Then let them come," I answered. "I'm not scared of them."

Then he changed tack and offered me about 10 million francs in Belgian money if I'd let him win in front of his own people. I refused. The only option left open to him was to start the sprint from a long way out. I didn't let this put me off my line and I jumped past him easily on my 52 x 12. I was the world champion. Fourth time lucky. Immediately after the race, Merckx came to congratulate me. Even he had to concede that on the strength of my performances during that season I was a worthy holder of the rainbow jersey.

Maertens' only regret: not to have been received by the King of the Belgians, as Merckx had been, and to have been sent a telegram instead. But the team did get through 100,000 Belgian francs' worth of champagne.

1977
The Moser mystery

It had the smell of burning rubber, as professional riders put it. Meaning that brakes went on at the finish to be sure that someone else won the race. Didi Thurau denies it. "I wanted to win as well, of course I did," he said of the 1977 world championship in San Cristobal, Venezuela. But the fact remains that he was ahead of the field with Francesco Moser when, with seven kilometers to go, Moser flatted. It was the moment the crowd expected him to flee for a certain gold medal, at the very least to keep riding at the same speed. But, instead, he hesitated and to everyone's astonishment, perhaps even Moser's, he let the Italian catch him. And then Moser won and became world champion.

There was no shortage of deep breaths.

"If I'd been richer, I'd have been world champion instead," Bernard Hinault said darkly.

"Very odd indeed," said Jacques Anquetil on his radio commentary.

"But normally Thurau is a man who really wants to win," said Peter Post, his manager at Raleigh.

The crowd went home discontented, feeling cheated. If Moser had paid to win the title then the least Thurau could have done was make it less obvious. This was a bike race, not professional wrestling. But then another story emerged, one that said not that Moser had paid to win but that Thurau had been paid to lose.

In 1977 Thurau had ridden for Raleigh. He'd had an exceptional year, with five stages in the Tour de France. But perhaps he had asked too much to stay at Raleigh and the notoriously cautious Post had declined to pay it or the ice-cream company, IJsboerke, had offered him more to move south into Belgium to bring coherence into a team which never met its potential.

In that story, IJsboerke had paid so much for a transfer in 1978 that it had no wish to see its new man in a rainbow jersey. For that money, Staf Janssens, the sponsor, wanted him clearly in the blue and yellow of an IJsboerke jersey. It was neither the first nor the last time such a thing happened. But Janssens lost his money because Thurau was never the same again. He looked more at ease opening supermarkets and appearing on television than he was out in the rain on his bike.

He finished the 1979 Tour three-quarters of an hour behind the best. He raced intermittently on the road and faded out of cycling while riding six-days on the track. He fell foul of dope tests and in 1989 he told *Bild* he'd taken amphetamine, testosterone and cortisone throughout his career. He was fined 20,000 marks in 1998 for forgery. In 2012, he was fined €39,900 for embezzling money meant for his father's nursing.

A man who looked like an angel turned out to be anything but.

1980
The world badgered

The one thing that everyone "knew" about the circuit at Sallanches in 1980 was that it was designed for Bernard Hinault. Isn't that just what the French would do: come up with a kidney-rupturing circuit that only a Frenchman could master? Typical! Well, if that was true, it was dispensing with a lot of ordinary human frailty. Not least because Hinault had abandoned the Tour de France only weeks earlier, sneaking out through the kitchens of his hotel in Pau to vanish into the night because of a hurting knee.

Cycling's World Championships

Nevertheless, Sallanches was neither a city nor a course like all the others. The locals knew about world championships because Jan Janssen had won the pro race and Eddy Merckx the amateur there in 1964. And the course wriggled in the foothills of Mont Blanc, which glowered down on mere humans like the mountains in the Pellos cartoons of the 1960s, lifting the hammers of exhaustion to bring down on their shoulders, and there wasn't a moment of rest worth the name. Apart from everything else, it had the côte de Domancy, a climb of nearly three kilometers at an average of eight per cent and moments at fifteen.

"That hill isn't what you'd normally expect in a world championship," Francesco Moser complained.

When it wasn't hard going up, it was winding and dangerously slippery in the rain going down.

Hinault took it and his reputation seriously. He saw Mariano Martinez attack and let him and two others gain as much as 2 minutes 50 seconds before stretching his own legs, to see who was man enough to follow. Martinez was absorbed by the peloton after 116 kilometers away. And then Hinault ground his teammates into the ground by insisting that they set a terrible pace to demoralize the strongest and destroy the rest. They obliged because they'd been promised a bonus if one of them won and another if that was Hinault. And then, at 150 kilometers on the 13th climb of the côte de Domancy, Hinault accelerated definitively and took Michel Pollentier, Jørgen Marcussen, Robert Millar and Gibi Baronchelli with him. A little behind them, an unknown American, Jonathon Boyer.

One by one they fell by the wayside. Baronchelli began refusing to share turns at the front with Hinault and then became the last to crack, in the last half lap. Hinault immediately took a minute out of him. The third man, Juan Fernandez of Spain, was at four minutes, leading in a group which had Boyer in fifth place and Roger De Vlaeminck, no less, in seventh.

Hinault won alone, satisfied with his personal war with Richard Marillier, the national team selector. Hinault never forgot how there were no French riders left at Ostuni when he looked round for their support. He had to look after his own chances and finished outside the medals and anonymously in sixth place. A war of words had then broken out, sometimes publicly, and Marillier was badgered into waiting for a properly demanding course and then picking a team worthy of what faced them. And to put Hinault at its head. That was one of the reasons that so many had been convinced that the circuit had been chosen simply so Hinault and the French could tear the world in two on their home soil.

Which they did.

1981
Freddy: the fall and rise and fall

No one had a more enigmatic career than Freddy Maertens. He could go from more than 50 wins in a season, including tour stages and a world championship, to nothing and then come back to another world championship.

The conclusion that many came to was that the rise and fall came with his growing and lessening dependence on drugs. But Maertens is strikingly open about that and many other subjects, sometimes admitting things that many riders wouldn't mention. And of drugs, he says: "Yes, I have to say that I took them. That happened to me just as it happened to all racing cyclists, but no more than anyone else. That's not the explanation. The explanation is in the fragile life that a champion lives and the daily problems that it brings."

The problems, specifically, were a huge tax bill that took 30 years to pay and the absence first of his dominating father and then of the dominating Lomme Driessens. In 1981 Maertens and Driessens were reunited at Boule d'Or, the last team in Europe to be sponsored by a cigarette company. Driessens took control of Maertens' life and found him accountants and lawyers to lift the weight of dealing with the tax office. And he pushed him into riding the world championship in Prague.

"The world championship was the one I really wanted to win," he said. "That didn't mean I ignored the others. But for the championship, first I *had* to be selected. And in Belgium there are always people left out of the team scandalously. That year, it looked as though everything was set up for Roger De Vlaeminck to win and so it wasn't certain that I'd get picked. So I had to prove that I had to be selected, by my results until the end of August. And on top of that, even despite my differences with Roger De Vlaeminck—and they were often exaggerated—I'd be prepared to sacrifice my chances and ride for him if he was in front."

Cycling's World Championships

There were still around 70 riders together when the bell sounded, including Bernard Hinault, who'd chased up to join them in his national championship jersey. Sven-Åke Nilsson of Sweden tried a long lonely ride in his blue and yellow jersey, but the Italians and Belgians worked behind him to bring up Francesco Moser and Maertens respectively. They left Nilsson to die and die he did.

Thirty men remained on the last climb, Beppe Saronni now moving up for Italy. Maertens had asked one of the Italians what his team had planned. The Italian replied: "If Moser can get away with riders who aren't as fast as him, he becomes our top man. As long as this group stays together, we're all riding for Saronni." So, with a sprint looking inevitable, Maertens knew whose wheel to pick. He could win—but only if he was over his demons. The Italians took no chances and led the little bunch into the last straight. But for the moment, no sign of Maertens.

"A kilometer out, I played dead," he said. "I stayed back in 20th place."

Gibi Baronchelli rode at a leg-tearing pace to hold Moser and now, increasingly, Saronni in the best spots. Baronchelli led into the last 400 meters with Saronni on his wheel. He swung aside and Saronni came through at such a speed that he looked unbeatable. But Maertens picked his 52 x 13—he was too tired to use the 12 sprocket—and went even faster and came by on his right, continuing down the finish straight with both arms raised until he saw his wife, Carine, running into the road from the right to hug him.

"Are you sure you've won? Are you sure you've won?", she kept shouting over the noise. The commentary was in Czech and all she'd understood were references to Bernard Hinault. Maertens got his rainbow jersey and his gold medal but not the bonus he said Boule d'Or had promised him, nor the Fiat Panda and a kitchen he thought he had won.

Saronni said he had never seen Maertens as a threat. Maertens said of Saronni that he'd made an elementary error: starting his sprint too early and into a headwind.

Curiously, local reporters were more interested that Eric Heiden had been there. Czechoslovakia had no professional cyclists and professional cycling was of interest only to enthusiasts. But Heiden had won five gold medals in skating at the previous year's Olympics and then seven in the world championship. It was he they wanted to see. And they wanted news of his sister, Beth, not because she'd won the world road championship the previous summer but because she too had won world skating championships, in 1978 and 1979.

As for Maertens, the devils returned. He won only two races from 1982 to when he retired after 1987.

1982
Revolution in the ranks

It wasn't likely that anybody was going to outsprint Beppe Saronni near the horse-racing town of Goodwood in southern England. Not even Sean Kelly, who was there beside him. But nobody could have guessed that Saronni would get the chance thanks not to other Italians but to two Americans who didn't like each other, one of whom didn't even consider himself in an American team.

The USA was so backward in international cycling that the nine riders it named for Goodwood were just about the only professionals it had and, even then, only six turned up. They'd been told they'd get no expenses to travel and so most were riders who lived in Europe anyway.

They included Jonathan Boyer, the first American to ride the Tour de France and the man who'd finished fifth to Bernard Hinault at Sallanches, and the younger and more talented Greg LeMond who was taking Boyer's limelight. They were both in the three dozen left at the front as the championship approached the hill just before the finish. The Italians were keeping the speed high to prevent anyone coming by Saronni, their star sprinter. Boyer knew he had no chance against Saronni, Kelly or several others in the group and so he attacked alone as the hill began.

Boyer wasn't a worry but Saronni wouldn't risk chasing because he'd take Kelly with him and the Irishman would ride by him. What he didn't know was that Kelly, in his own estimation, was young and green and had "chased everything that moved and used up most of my energy before I got near the finish." In that moment when the race was locked, it was unpicked by the last rider Saronni would have expected: Boyer's teammate, LeMond. Photos of the moment that LeMond set off in chase show Saronni looking towards him and smiling.

Cycling's World Championships

Boyer, who seriously thought he was to become world champion, had the ignominy of seeing another American sweep by him. Saronni was on his wheel and Kelly behind him, taken by surprise. Saronni then sprinted unstoppably and won by five seconds, with LeMond second and Boyer alone and disillusioned in tenth place.

Boyer saw LeMond's move as treachery. LeMond, by contrast, said the USA had done nothing, that there had been no expenses, no manager, no masseur. There was no contract with the home country and none with other members of the team. And that included Boyer, whom he wasn't alone in disliking. What complicated the ethics was that the world championship was also the *national* championship. Whichever American finished first would be his country's champion. So it followed that Americans would ride not for each other but as opponents.

LeMond said he had pointed that out to American administrators and to other riders but had been overruled.

Decades later, Boyer told the author, Richard Moore: "I asked Greg why. He said that he didn't care who won, as long as it wasn't me; that I didn't deserve to win, didn't deserve the publicity, that I'd done nothing all year. It was a deliberate move on his part. Greg didn't like the fact that I got any publicity. He wanted his own publicity; he wanted to do it for himself."

Boyer raced until 1987. In 1997 he became involved with an under-age girl at his church. He was jailed for a year. He now lives in Rwanda.

1982
First BMX championships

BMX is one of three branches of cycling that openly ape motorcycling. The others are cycle speedway, using bomb sites to mimic motorcycle speedway, and cycle trials, which copy a motorcycling skill challenge. BMX, from the 1970s onwards, copied motorcycle scrambling, from the word "moto-cross" in the name right down to the heavy helmet and extravagant padding and protection. Whereas cycle speedway grew from youthful exuberance, BMX has been criticized as commercial manipulation of childhood enjoyment. It arrived without trace.

BMX was quickly taken on by the UCI. The origins are as casual as cycle-speedway but within a few years there was a governing body in the USA, where the sport started, and by April 1981 there was an International BMX Federation and the first world championships were in 1982. BMX has been part of the UCI since January 1993.

There are two branches. BMX supercross, which is part of the Olympics, has eight riders on a 350 meter circuit of hillocks, banked corners and flat sections. They set off from a raised starting gate. BMX freestyle is a test of technique rather than speed, a series of jumps judged on difficulty, originality and style.

Recent men's Supercross winners have come from Australia, Britain, France, Latvia and the USA. The sport is unusual in having always had championships for women. Recent winners have been from Colombia, France, Britain, New Zealand and Holland.

1983
Not America's; it's *mine!*

When Hugh Porter was world champion at the professional pursuit, word had it that he slept in a condemned apartment near the docks in Ghent rather than pay for anything better. Whether the story is actually true, it matches every story you hear about Porter and his eagerness not to spend more than he had to even when he was at the peak of his profession.

The opposite applied to Greg LeMond. He stayed in a four-star hotel beside Lake Constance, a lake on the Rhine that borders Germany, Switzerland and Austria, and then moved to one still better: the Bad Schachen just inside Germany. Why? Because America's first cycling coach, the one who spotted LeMond as a junior, used to say in broken English (he came from Poland): "Before big race you must stay in good hotel and eat well."

There was no bigger race for LeMond than the world championship of 1983. And yet, despite taking Eddy Borysewicz's advice, he had a bad night's sleep. And on that he tackled 18 laps of 15 kilometers for a total of 270 kilometers on the southern bank of the lake, in Switzerland. Anybody who completed the race would have climbed 4,058 meters, because any course starting by a lake and returning to it repeatedly was going to have a lot of uphill to ride.

Renault had promised LeMond $25,000 if he won. He'd signed his contract with the team, the first he had as a professional, on the last day of the Tour de France in 1980. The bonus works out at close to $60,000 today. Jonathan Boyer, who accused LeMond of treachery the previous year in England, was also in the team; if anybody had promised him a bonus then it was academic because he wasn't going to win and, had he shown any hint that he might, the clash of personality and ambition hadn't dwindled enough to make it likely.

Phil Anderson, a toothy Australian who had been LeMond's training partner at home in Kortrijk, made an early effort and covered some of the early moves in a deal with LeMond. He was never seen again. LeMond, on the other hand, didn't show himself at all, other than by throwing up his food in the first hour because of his nerves. He was invisible until only 40 kilometers, about an hour of racing, were left. And then he attacked, passing the prickly and skinny Brit, Robert Millar, but taking with him the Italian favorite, Moreno Argentin, and the Spaniard, Faustino Ruperez. A blue cordon then appeared across the front of the main field as the Italian *azzuri* set up a defensive wall to protect their man. It was in their interest: they were on $10,000 not just if Argentin won but if *any* Italian could do it.

But their money vanished in the Swiss hills. Argentin was dropped on the main rise and crossed the line in tears. He would have a lot of explaining to do. "From that day on, he hated me," LeMond said. "I think he got so much crap from the Italian team for working with me and then getting dropped that he took it out on me."

LeMond, having got rid of an Italian, now sensed that he'd have little trouble with the Spaniard. He bent his cranks and rode off alone, finishing 1 minute 11 seconds ahead of anyone else.

LeMond, so smiling and friendly in appearance, had crocodile teeth. "People have said that my victory is a victory for American cycling," he said next day. "I fashioned this win my own way, and the title belongs to nobody but me. There are lots of coaches in the United States who have good ideas on training, but they know nothing about the difficulties of actual competition."

At 22, LeMond still had a lot to learn about diplomacy and not making unnecessary enemies.

Les Woodland

1984
Twigg blossoms

Nobody pretended the final of the 1984 women's pursuit in Barcelona would be between anyone but Jeannie Longo of France and Rebecca Twigg of the USA. Twigg had won as an unknown at Leicester in 1982 and in 1983 she came second in the world road race in Switzerland. Matching her in the final against a rider with a near-identical background but a lot more experience was going to produce a battle worth seeing.

Longo had come third three times running, in 1981, then to Twigg at Leicester in 1982, kept from better by another American, Connie Carpenter, then again in 1983, when Carpenter won.

Jacques Duniecq's assessment was: "From the opening round of this thinly contested event, it was obvious that the final would be between Twigg and Longo, barring accidents. It wasn't just that they had put up the fastest times in the qualifying round; Twigg was the reigning champion and Longo the rider with amazing form, and most of the others had been around for long enough without winning anything significant."

The two were a contrast on the track, Longo with a plugging style, Twigg taller and more fluid. Twigg took the lead from the start but she had less than a second after 1,000 meters, a third of the distance. But she went on to finish in a championship record time.

Twigg won the world pursuit six times—1982, 1984, 1985, 1987, 1993 and 1995—and also came second in the Olympic road race in 1984. She went to the University of Washington, where she lived in Seattle, when she was 14. Longo finally did win the pursuit, in Colorado Springs in 1986, when she put Twigg into second place before her own fans. And she won again in 1988 and 1989.

1984
First unicycle championships

It's called Unicon, it's been held every two years since Syracuse in the USA in 1984, and it's the world unicycling championship. It has skill and artistic competitions but it also downhill racing, street competitions, hockey and basketball.

Cycling's World Championships

The world record for an hour on a unicycle is 32 kilometers and the record for the high jump, 1.4 meters. The sport is administered by the International Unicycling Federation in Oakland, California.

1985
Jeannie arrives

Jeannie Longo won her first world road championship at Montello, Italy, and became the most dominant rider in women's racing until the arrival of Marianne Vos in 2006.

Longo won the road race in 1985, 1986, 1987, 1989 and 1995, and the time trial in 1995, 1996, 1997 and 2001. She also won 31 national championships. If she were a man, she said in 2005, she would be living in Monaco and "my only worry would be paying less tax."

In 2011, Longo was voted France's favorite athlete in a poll run by *L'Équipe*, beating the rugby player, Sébastien Chabal, and the rally driver, Sébastian Loeb. *France-Soir* said it was because she "is seen as an uncomplicated girl, a woman of 53 who admitted recently that she didn't even own a cell phone."

Rudi Altig, who made a television program with her as they cycled round Scotland together, decided that she had *"une personnalité bien trempée."* The expression means that she is inclined to speak her mind, sometimes loudly. The words came high in a portrait of her in *France-Soir*. When a reporter asked her about allegations that she had used EPO—on which she was cleared—she answered: "If you print scandalous rubbish like that, you're bastards."

In 2003 Longo said: "I get on well with young riders. I feel at home with them." But her former teammate, Nathalie Hervier, called her "very reserved, very distant, rarely mixing with others. She's not easy to live with, even in races." One of those young riders referred to her throughout a television interview not as "Jeannie" but "Madame Longo."

A British rider recalled her punching her way through the peloton, literally, to get to the front.

She conducted a battle with the French federation over the make of pedals she was prepared to ride and in 1997 she was fined 50,000 Swiss francs for adding advertising to her world championship jersey on the day she won it.

But for all the criticism, she proved herself where it mattered: in races.

1986
First trials championships

The trials world championship is another that most cycling fans have no idea exists. Like speedway and BMX, it copies motorcycling. It's the only branch of cycling in which speed counts for nothing. The challenge is to follow a tricky course without dabbing, as motorcyclists call it: putting a foot to the ground. It began in Europe in the 1970s as part of motorcycling but moved to the UCI in 1985. The first world championship was the following year. The most successful nations are Belgium, France, Germany, Spain and Switzerland. Championships are often combined with mountain-bike races. There are events for men and women.

1987
Singing in the rain

The summer of 1987 was one the cherubic Irishman, Stephen Roche, will never forget. How could he? He won the Tour de France, the Giro d'Italia and the world championship.

The championship road race of September 1987 began in heavy rain, at Villach, in southern Austria. Irishmen had won bronze medals—Sean Kelly in England in 1982 and Roche in Switzerland in 1983. But that was the best they'd done since 1962, when Shay Elliott came second. Ireland had talent but never a team strong enough to exploit it.

Roche's win in the Tour led many to dismiss his chances at Villach. Georges Speicher and Louison Bobet had won the Tour and the championship in the same year but only Eddy Merckx had won the Giro, Tour and the world championship. Roche would never have made the comparison and certainly nobody else did. He spent the week before Villach telling reporters that he was going to ride for Kelly.

But that was before he saw the circuit. The papers had all said it was flat, which is why Roche thought Kelly had the better chance. But instead, he said, "it was a circuit for strong men, essentially like Sean and Moreno Argentin, but I knew that I would go OK.

"On the long hill at the start of the lap, I went as hard as I could go. Sean was on my wheel. I wanted to put the other sprinters under pressure but I could not believe it when I looked behind at the top of the hill and saw that there were only 10 or 11 guys still with me. I did push the speed up but I had no idea that it was fast enough to get rid of about 60 riders. Getting the field of potential winners down to 12 suited Sean and me well."

By now Kelly and Moreno Argentin were sizing each other for a sprint. Roche and the rest stood no chance against either and wanted a break that would drop one or both. Roche said: "I knew that if I was in a sprint I was likely to get fourth or fifth with only an outside possibility of bronze. After the year that I had enjoyed, a bronze medal at the world championship was not worth winning and it was obvious that I had to attack."

So 500 meters from the line he attacked. He sprinted through a narrow gap beside the barriers on the left of the road. Everyone hesitated, even Argentin, who waited too long and came second. It hadn't been the most animated of races, but then perhaps simply the historical significance of winning the Tour, the Giro and the world championship compensated for much.

1989
Back from the dead

In 1989, Greg LeMond became world champion at Chambéry, in the hilly Savoie region of France near Mont Blanc. That summer, he had won the Tour de France. And yet in April, 1987, he had been accidentally shot in the back while hunting turkeys with his uncle and brother-in-law in California. The three men had gone their own way and lost track of each other. A gun fired so close to LeMond that he thought his own had gone off by mistake. When he realized it hadn't, he stood up to see who had fired. It was then that 60 pellets hit him in his right lung, kidney and liver. A helicopter eventually lifted him to hospital.

Nobody expected him to ride again but next year he began again, but crashed and rarely appeared until August. It was easy to write him off.

"Every race I entered from when I got shot felt like, from a press perspective, it was do-or-die," he said. "Even when I got shot, I received some hate mail that was so mean. People saying 'Oh, you got what you deserved, you shouldn't have been hunting.'" Yet in 1989 he won the Tour de France after a race-long tussle with Laurent Fignon was settled by just eight seconds.

The world championship was only weeks after the Tour, 17 times up the col de Montagnole. It was so hard and the weather so bad that LeMond, who hadn't wanted to ride in the first place, thought about stopping each time he passed the pits. Only in the last third of the race did he start feeling "unblocked", as he put it.

Clearly it didn't show even on the last lap, because Fignon set off on the final climb to catch the leaders—Steven Rooks, Dimitri Konyshev and his own teammate, Thierry Claveyrolat—only to discover a much revived LeMond on his wheel. A world championship would compensate Fignon for the humiliation on the Champs Elysées in the Tour but now here was his tormentor right behind him.

Fignon could have eased up rather than go through it all over again. But while the American had no helpers in the break, Fignon had the little climber, Thierry Claveyrolat (known as "cotter pin" because of his size).

The leaders rode through the streets of Chambéry. Fignon attacked under the red triangle of the final kilometer and the others lined out behind him. Still the rain fell. Behind, three riders slid off on a bend. Scan Kelly was the obvious pick, biding his time two places from the back. And then out of the last left bend, LeMond sprinted up the left of the road and crossed the line with his right arm in the air, barely ahead of the rest, his mouth open.

Chapter 8: 1990 – 2005

Mountain bikes, time trialists, messengers, lots more championships

1990
First mountain bike championships

The origins of mountain-bike racing are hazy because it evolved from riders riding old bikes down hills, mainly in the USA. The National Off-Road Bicycle Association, founded in California in January 1983, is said to be the sport's first association.

The old bikes had 26-inch wheels, which had dropped out of common use. The better bikes produced later copied those of the pioneers and the 26-inch wheel was reborn.

Of the original bikes, Charlie Kelly wrote in *Bicycling* that they were "usually old Schwinns, although a few other rugged species are included. Highly modified, most are five- or ten-speeds with front and rear drum brakes, motorcycle brake levers, motocross bars, and the biggest knobby tires available. A few reactionaries still cling to their one or two-speed coaster brake machines, but drum brakes and ten speeds seem to be the wave of the future. The machines are referred to as clunkers, bombers or cruisers."

Historian Jim McGurn wrote: "Adults on motorcycles and youths on utility bicycles made a sport of careering down steep hillsides, and then being transported back up in a truck. When motorcycles were banned by the authorities, the men switched to utility bicycles, which they thought would be stronger than light touring cycles. The utility cycles proved too weak and their back-pedal brakes overheated. This led to a series of design changes, by amateurs and then by professional cycle makers, which resulted in a rugged but light machine with appropriately fat tires, 15 or more gears, powerful cantilever brakes, oversized tubing and wide handlebars: generally known as the mountain-bike."

The first cross-country championship, at Durango, Colorado, USA, was won by Ned Overend, an American born in Taiwan. Another American, John Tomac, won the following year but from then on the sport was dominated by Europeans. The most successful is the Frenchman, Julien Absalon, who won every year from 2004–2007 and again in 2014.

Mountain-bike racing developed later and separately from cyclo-cross, with which it shares similarities. The differences, though, are more noticeable: courses are trickier and often narrower and riders are not allowed to change bikes during a race.

1991 and 1992
Italian rebound

Things looked unpromising for Gianni Bugno in 1989. He was 25, he'd never lived up to the hope put in him by still more Italians longing for another Coppi, and he looked like being just another talented bottle-carrier. And then he won Milan–San Remo in 1990. "That was the key year," he said, crediting the teaching of Gianluigi Stanga, who managed the Château d'Ax team that he joined in 1988. "I learned how to do everything. I had to lose, lose, lose, then start to win. If I did nothing in 1990, I was finished as a champion, an idol. I was never going to make it as a good rider."

His therapy included listening to Mozart to calm his nerves, especially about going downhill. In 1991 he also beat Steven Rooks and Miguel Indurain to win the world championship. He won in good weather at Stuttgart from a four-man break that had been away for around an hour. The Colombian, Alvaro Meija, made half-hearted attempts to lead the others or provoke a move in the last few hundred meters but Bugno sprinted early and won without challenge.

Beating Indurain was a big mental step because he could never do it in the Tour de France, where the Spaniard laid a dead hand across the race and won because of his talent in the time trials. Of the 1991 Tour, Bugno said: "My training that year was mainly addressed to the Tour, but Indurain was stronger than me. Looking back there is nothing I could have done to beat him." But there was better to come. The 1992 championship was in Benidorm, a vacation city of high-rise hotels on the Spanish south coast.

Bugno had finished second to Indurain in the 1991 Tour and third to him—and behind another Italian, Claudio Chiappucci—in 1992. Now he had a chance to belittle Indurain in Spain itself. And that's exactly what he did.

Indurain, Chiappucci and the Swiss, Tony Rominger, spent the race watching each other, and a group of about 40 arrived at the finish after a long, tense ride along the beach edge. Bugno won from a long sprint again, Laurent Jalabert behind him but unable to advance, and the rest a couple of lengths back. Bugno had successfully defended his rainbow jersey, the first to do it since Rik van Looy in 1961.

Bugno retired at the end of 1998 to work as a helicopter pilot, flying in the Tour of Lombardy and the Giro d'Italia. He had no regrets about his past and any races he'd failed to win, except perhaps Paris–Roubaix. "Talking after a race is easy," he said, "saying 'I could have done this or that to win.' But, when you're a bike rider, it's better to talk with your legs."

But there *was* something to regret. He was investigated and then cleared on appeal in Italy on a charge of sporting fraud related to drug-taking. But then Belgian police took such an interest in the Three Days of De Panne in 1999 and a package of amphetamines there that one of the stages was canceled. The delivery company, DHL, had told the police it had suspicions about the parcel, which it said had been addressed to Bugno, who was working for the Mapei team. Riders were questioned but cleared. Bugno, however, was summoned to a court hearing in Kortrijk in 2001. In 2003 he was fined a little less than €5,000 and given a suspended jail sentence of six months for buying and having five bottles of amphetamines.

1993
First bicycle messenger championships

There have been national championships for postmen, soldiers and even butchers. So what more logical than a world championship for cycle-messengers?

The first was in Berlin in 1993, chosen because that's where the organizers, Achim Beier and Stefan Klessman happened to live. The championship has been held in cities in Europe, North America, Australia and even in Japan and Guatemala. The challenge differs every year but is always formed from challenges that cycle-messengers are said to face every day at work. The main race demands participants deliver messages to addresses revealed only at the start. One of several subsidiary contests is to produce the longest skid.

The first winners were Andy Schneider of Germany and Ursi Haenny of Switzerland.

1994
First time trial championship

The end of the national team time trial in 1994 brought an individual time trial as replacement. The first winner was Chris Boardman, of Britain. The length and nature of the course changes every year, although it's usually between 40 and 60 kilometers without unusual hills.

1994
First para championships

Paracycling has had world championships since 1994. The UCI took control from the International Paralympic Committee in 2007. There are road races and a time trial for men and a hand-cycling relay. The track races are a tandem sprint for men, a mixed team sprint, a 500-meter or 1-kilometer time trial and a pursuit. Riders are grouped according to disabilities.

1995
First masters championships

Masters racing, previously known in some countries as veteran racing, is a product not only of people living longer but of staying active for decades longer than they used to. The first championship, in Manchester in 1965, had 100 riders from seven countries riding races for men older than 60 and women aged 30–39 and more than 40. American Nick Chenowth, 43, came within 0.5 seconds of the Manchester track record for 200 meters set by world champion Marty Nothstein. Age, however, does not always bring wisdom. In 2002, Chenowth ended up in jail after admitting bumping up expense claims to his employer by nearly $1.3 million.

The UCI formally recognized masters racing in 1987 and the age categories widened. Many of the riders are unknown to wider cycling but some are faces from the past. The over-65 points champion in 1998 was Canada's Norman Sheil, who won 40 years after taking his second world amateur pursuit championship. In 2001, the Australian six-day rider Danny Clark beat his 10-year-old personal best in the sprint.

1996
First bicycle polo championships

It took a long time for bicycle polo to have a recognized world championship. It was back in Ireland in October, 1891, that the editor of *The Irish Cyclist*, Richard Mecredy, hit on abandoning horses and riding bicycles instead. He'd been a serious rider; he won the Irish one-, two- and four-mile championships in 1886 and, in total, nine gold medals. He was always open to novel ideas and he helped organize the Gordon Bennett car race in Ireland after Britain said it wouldn't allow car racing on the road.

How he came to think of bicycle polo is a mystery. But the first recorded match was at Scalp, in County Wicklow, Ireland, between Rathclaren Rovers and the Ohne Hast (German for "no hurry") cycling club on October 4, 1891. It was enough of a success that Mercredy published the rules in his paper at the end of the month.

Bicycle polo spread to Britain, France, and the USA. The first international was between Ireland and England in 1901. Seven years later Ireland beat Germany in a demonstration game at the London Olympics. The leading nations now are India (world champions 1996–2001) and Canada (2002, 2003 and 2006).

1996
The end of amateurs and professionals

Cycling wasn't alone in struggling with the concept of amateurs and professionals. The whole Olympic movement accepted that amateur competition had risen to the point that it could no longer match the ideal of enthusiasts training at weekends and in the evening after work. Few western amateurs good enough to ride had conventional jobs and those from some eastern European countries certainly didn't.

The distinction between amateurs and professionals was abandoned in 1996 and cycling held championships instead for under-23s, over-23s, and juniors.

2000
Romans with a sad ending

Latvia. You know: that place you can't quite find on the map. Somewhere east of Norway, maybe, or going that way anyway.

Romāns Vainšteins has had that problem ever since he became a cyclist. That and explaining to people how to spell his name and how to find those dinky accents on their keyboards. He also came from a country which had refused him help to prepare for the Olympics because, as the *Baltic Times* said, in Latvia "cyclists are considered more of a nuisance than athletes" and because he wanted to train in Italy instead.

Well, in 2000 at Plouay in France, Vainšteins became the first world road champion for Latvia, crossing the line in his orange jersey and throwing up both arms with a lead no further than you could spit. Behind him, a bunch of 23.

It was a sprint finish and nobody rated that or Vainšteins that highly. He had turned professional only two years earlier and he won only one race in the following three years. He dropped out of the sport in 2004 because nobody would pay him what he thought he was worth. The curse of the rainbow jersey—and more on that later—had struck.

2002
Legs bigger than a Spice Girl's waist

You'd be annoyed not to know it: it's four inches further round one of Chris Hoy's legs than it is around Victoria Beckham's waist. And in case you've spent your life, quite reasonably, more interested in Hoy than Beckham, she was the dark-haired one of the Spice Girls, the so-called girl-power group that was supposed to become "bigger than the Beatles."

Cycling's World Championships

Hoy's thighs are each 27 inches in circumnavigation. That's the same size, as it happens, as one of Hoy's rivals, Grégory Baugé of France, but Hoy's look bigger because he's 12 kilograms heavier. Those legs, starting in 2002, took Hoy to eleven world championship gold medals, eight silver and six bronze, all in ten years. He is one of only two cyclists knighted by the Queen: the other is Bradley Wiggins, Britain's first winner of the Tour de France. But it wasn't the Tour that inspired him to race. It was the film, ET. He was six and much taken by a scene at the end in which kids on BMX bikes are chased by the police.

"I just thought, wow, I'd like to give that a go."

He raced in BMX from the age of seven to fourteen and was for a while ranked ninth in the world. He tried rowing and rugby and then began track bike racing in 1993. His first gold medals were at Copenhagen in 2002, in the kilometer, beating the world record holder, Arnaud Tournant of France, and in the team sprint.

Hoy won the kilometer in 2004, 2006 and 2007. He abandoned the kilo when the Olympics dropped it and took instead to the keirin, which he won in 2007, 2008, 2010 and 2012. In 2007, he fell short of the world kilometer record by 0.005 seconds. And yet he came close to throwing it all in. He lived the student life while he was taking maths and physics at St Andrews University and got a taste for beer and banter.

"But at the end of the first year I realized that if I stayed up there for another three years, I wasn't going to touch my bike. I wasn't going to have the chance to explore how far I could go with cycling," he said. "It was a tough decision because I had some really good friends. But I stepped away from that and moved back to Edinburgh, so I could be closer to the track and my teammates."

Hoy is a product of British cycling's coaching at Manchester velodrome. Baugé, a Parisian who won the world sprint in 2009, 2010 and 2012, said enviously: "They have cameras everywhere and they can see how riders develop, how they handle the bankings. It's crazy what they have." And Hoy agrees. He came from a system that looked not for a ten per cent improvement in one area but a one per cent improvement in ten.

"You wouldn't think that shaving your legs is a big issue," Hoy said. "A few hairs, what is that going to do? But when you get into the wind tunnel, you can pick up literally little tufts of hair, a wrinkle in your clothing. If you move your hands slightly it'll pick up on the aerodynamic drag.

"You have the people there who work full-time to make you as aerodynamic as possible. You have the coaches there to get you in the best possible physical condition. The psychologists to talk through your mental approach. All these tiny little things, you have to become a bit obsessive about it."

He now has more Olympic medals than any other cyclist in history and more than anyone in any sport in Britain. Not that fame is everything. In 2014, he was asked to identify himself before being allowed to enter the stadium in Glasgow that had been named after him.

2005
Grass roots

At thirteen, Victoria Pendleton used to race on a track laid out on grass like a school sports ground. That was at a rally held each year in Mildenhall, in eastern England, and even then she showed talent. In 2005 she won the sprint in Los Angeles and became only the third British woman in 40 years to become a world cycling champion. The others were Beryl Burton and Mandy Jones, who won the road race in England in 1982.

Pendleton looked more a pursuiter than a sprinter, slightly built and weighing only 60 kilograms. She characteristically rode at the back and then down the banking and past her opponent. She won gold medals at every world championship from 2005 to 2010 except 2006, when she was second in the sprint to the Russian, Natalia Tsylinskaya. Pendleton won again in 2012.

In 2007 she won the sprint, the keirin and, with Shanaze Reade, the team sprint. In 2008 she won the sprint, the team sprint, again with Reade. She won the sprint again in 2009, although her rides against her Dutch opponent, Willy Kanis, needed photos to see she had won. Pendleton was known for bursting into tears and this was one of those occasions.

Kanis rode BMX in summer, becoming world champion in 2005 and 2006, and the track and bobsleigh in winter.

Cycling's World Championships

Pendleton won the sprint again in 2010, beating Guo Shuang of China. Her roughest sprint win came in 2012 when she fell in her first heat of the semifinal against Anna Meares of Australia. Meares was relegated in the second heat for leaving her lane. Pendleton won the decider in a photo finish before beating Simona Krupeckaitė of Lithuania in the final.

Chapter 9: 2006 – Present

The modern era. "Nobody's ever a hero in Belgium."

2006
Smiley Paolo

The fun thing about Paolo Bettini was that he combined Italian cycling's flamboyance with that of the population in general. How many winners have stood on the podium and sung their heart out to the sound of their anthem?

Bettini, a little, round-faced, smiling and short-haired man seemingly prepared to have a go at anything—including six-days, where he was so popular even with the opposition that they slowed down to avoid beating him by too much. So when he won the 2006 championship in Salzburg, he braked to a halt and lifted his bike so enthusiastically in celebration that he came close to throwing it in the air. And, because he was as popular with those he defeated as he was with his fans, the silver medalist, Erik Zabel, had to push through the crowd to hug him in congratulation.

And Bettini told reporters in turn: "He is such a great friend and bike rider, who deserves a lot of respect. I hope he will come back next year and win a world championship!"

The race had looked as though it would end in a bunch sprint. But one man made the difference. A Spaniard, Xavier Florencio, braked hard on the bend 500 meters before the line to split the field. Another Spaniard, Alejandro Valverde, took the cue and attacked. Braking in a bend or at the bottom of a hill to help a teammate is a well-worn tactic and Zabel and Bettini were too wily to let it happen. That it had all been planned all along became all the more obvious when Valverde, and none of the others, had a lead-out man with him: Samuel Sanchez.

But Valverde blundered. Worried about Zabel, the better sprinter, he came off Sanchez's wheel too early and faded before he reached the line, pushing too high a gear. Zabel saw it and sprinted on the left. But he too had gone too soon and in the end Bettini passed them all with less than 50 meters left. Another two seconds and they would have been swamped by the bunch.

Someone asked Bettini, at the post-race press conference, what more he hoped to achieve. The Tour of Flanders, he said, "but I don't know...maybe I'll try something new, like the track." He never did win the Tour of Flanders but he did win a race he didn't mention: he won the world championship the following year as well. And sure enough, he hung up his bike after winning the six-day at Milan in November 2008, having progressed from his first sight of the track at Grenoble, which scared him. He wished he had ridden the winter track sooner. "If more stars get out there and race the six-days," he said, "I'm convinced that they would see a serious jump in participation and return to their golden days."

And, he said, what better than training indoors each winter and being paid for it?

2009
Smiling down-under

Australia had never won a road pro championship before Mendrisio in 2009. Jack Hoobin won the amateur race in 1950 in Belgium but, among the professionals, Robbie McEwen's second to Mario Cipollini at Zolder in 2002 was as good as it had been. So maybe it was that unfamiliarity that led Cadel Evans to just about lift his left finger as he crossed the line and then to scratch his nose with the other hand. He was out of place.

As James Startt wrote for *Bicycling*: "He seemed stunned. Few picked him as a possible favorite since he, well, never wins. The French sports daily, *L'Équipe*, gave him a measly two stars out of five, on par with the modest French rider, Sylvain Chavanel, another rider who has trouble winning."

Cycling's World Championships

Evans had always been a puzzle in the uncomplicated, rarely deep-thinking world of professional cycling. Where most riders came from conventional middle-class backgrounds with little intellectualism beyond their quest for sports cars and trinkets, Evans grew up in an Aborigine community and wore a vest showing allegiance with Tibet. He lived in an area of Australia's Northern Territory where he sometimes saw nobody for days. His parents then took him to the Aboriginal community, "for the adventure", before separating soon afterward.

As an adult, he married an Italian gospel singer and pianist. In 2011, they adopted a one-year-old from Ethiopia. Little of this was typical of the riders around him and so maybe it was right that so unusual a man should win the world championship for a country that had never won it.

He rode away from the rest on the last hill, close to the end of a workmanlike 260-kilometer race. Evans broke away from Alexander Kolobnev of Russia and Spaniard Joaquin Rodriquez on the final climb of the Novazzano, and won by 27 seconds. He seemed quite unmoved by the experience and only on the podium did he show emotion, the tears starting.

"People have often treated me as a loser and I've accepted my criticisms," he said. "Sometimes it makes me sad because, when you finish, you've worked just as hard as the winner. Today the perseverance finally paid off."

2011
Dancing back to happiness

Not for close on half a century—46 years, to be exact—had Britain won the professional road championship. And then, in one of those details that journalists love, the drought was ended by a former ballroom dancer born not actually in Britain but in the neighboring independent state of the Isle of Man.

Ellan Vannin, as it's known locally, has a curious status. It is not Britain but a British dependency. It is not in the European Union but the Manx have EU passports headed not "United Kingdom" but "British Islands: Isle of Man."

You're probably getting the picture. It's complicated. And, anyway, Manx riders have licenses issued by British Cycling. Which is how

Les Woodland

Mark Cavendish won for Britain in a bunch sprint in Denmark in 2012. He beat Matt Goss of Australia, Germany's André Greipel and the Swiss, Fabian Cancellara. He was the first British winner since Tom Simpson in Spain in 1965. He'd been a long way back as the bunch entered the finish stretch but he pushed to the front and squeezed though a gap along by the barrier on the right of the road. From then on he couldn't be stopped.

He said: "We knew three years ago when this course was announced, that it could be good for us. We put a plan together to come with the best group of guys to this race and to come away from it with the rainbow jersey. It's been three years in the making. The guys have worked so hard throughout the season to get points so that we could have eight riders here and, as you just saw, they rode incredibly. I feel so, so proud."

And the ballroom dancing? Well, he went to Madigan's Dance School in Douglas for nine years and "just took to dancing", said his teacher, Janice Madigan. "He was fabulous. He is very competitive, very enthusiastic and always wanted to be the best. As a dancer he was fabulous. He has got stamina, very fast feet and strong legs. Before any competition he would know he was going out to win. He liked Latin American, jive and rumba, and even the more fuddy-duddy classical sequences."

He is better known, though, for outbursts far removed from the gentle world of sequins and patent leather shoes. Of a rider caught in a dope test, for instance, he said: "Patrik Sinkewitz? If I ever see him in the same peloton as me, I'll jump off my bike, straight on to him and kick the shit out of him."

2012
Gilbert the peace-maker

"Nobody's ever a hero in Belgium," Freddy Maertens once said. Meaning that however good you are, there's always someone to say you're not. Except that Philippe Gilbert was different. Not only did he not have the buzzing mosquito battle that Maertens and Eddy Merckx had, but like Merckx and unlike Maertens, he is neither clearly of the Dutch-speaking north or the French-speaking south. And if that seems unimportant then it's worth reading a history of Belgium.

True enough, his first language is French. But he comes from neither north nor south but the eastern extreme of Liège, which is itself a curiosity because it has an enclave in which the official language is neither French nor Dutch but German. So Gilbert spoke French and Dutch equally well with only a tiny accent to betray him. Like Merckx, he could be claimed by both sides and be embraced as a symbol of a future, socially united Belgium.

In 2012 he won the world championship just over the border in the hilly Limburg province of Holland, where the Amstel Gold Race wriggles. The race rode 105 kilometers through southern Limburg before starting ten laps of a circuit to complete 267 kilometers just beyond the Cauberg.

Gilbert attacked the final time up the Cauberg, where the Amstel finishes and which is 1.5-kilometer long climb and up to 12 percent, and won Belgium's first road championship title since Tom Boonen in Madrid in 2005. The race marked a turning, because he'd won only two races all season. But it was also made for him, since he'd won the Amstel in 2010 and 2011.

The Italians had wanted to get in first, sending Luca Paolini to lead out Vincenzo Nibali. At one moment there were four Belgians on Nibali's wheel. But the Italians went too soon and faded and Gilbert rode by on his big ring.

"The Belgians did outstanding work today," he said. "We deserved to win. I was well placed. I looked back quickly and then I took off."

2014
Pole position

Michal Kwiatkowski came out of nowhere to win under the rain in Spain in 2014. Well, that's what they tell you, anyway. Sure enough, there were far bigger names alongside him. And when a small fish wins beside sharks, you usually say he was lucky or that he profited from the hesitation of others.

Well, take a step back. Kwiatkowski isn't one of the first names on a list of likely winners, but he was European road champion in 2007 and time trial champion in 2008. A year later he was under-23 champion in Poland. If the others missed that, well, whose fault was that? The outcome was that Poland had its first professional road champion, and at 24, and that he won not in a sprint but by chasing up to the break and then riding away from it.

Poland had always favored Kwiatkowski, who'd told them in the morning that he could win, and his team chased the early escapees to limit the risk for him. By the last lap, the hours of rain had ended and Vasil Kiryienka, Alessandro De Marchi, Cyril Gautier and Michael Andersen had 40 seconds' lead, feeling more confident and starting to watch each other before the run-in to the line. But that was to the benefit of the Spanish, who didn't fancy being left back in the also-rans on their own soil, and then of the Italians. The opposition set off in a cross mood and the leaders had just 25 seconds with 13 kilometers to go. And that lead was steadily growing less.

The distance and the day-long rain was now telling. So were the climbs, including the Confederación. By the time the riders went up it for the last time, the break had only nine seconds. It was then that Kwiatkowski jumped the rest and reached the leaders. But instead of pausing and assessing the situation, he went straight by them, demoralizing them and leaving them to be caught by the rest.

It was good for the crowd watching on huge television screens beside the road but it was to the displeasure of everyone else. It was bad enough to be beaten by a star and it was forgivable to be forgotten in a mass sprint. But to have a young and barely known Pole teach you a lesson in courage wasn't on. Not in Spain, it wasn't, and a Spaniard, Joaquin Rodriguez, set off in chase and took five riders with him. Kwiatkowski had seven seconds with two kilometers to go. It looked tight. But there was just time enough and he held on to win by a single second. The photos made it look like a sprint, but they mislead: no world champion is more worthy than a man who attacks, passes the break and wins alone.

"I felt really good on the least lap," he said, clearly astonished at what had happened. "I went to the race to win and I took risks where others preferred to calculate, and I waited for the last climb. You know, two days ago I looked at the course when the under-23s were riding it and I told myself I could win. It's unbelievable!"

Kwiatkowski was the youngest world road champion since Óscar Freire in 1999, who was 23.

Epilogue

The curse of the rainbow jersey

It used to be that a rider had only to get his picture on the front of *Procycling* for something unpleasant to befall him. Much the same has been said of the rainbow jersey, which has often been the start of a barren period and sometimes worse. In the last 50 years…

Benoni Beheyt won in 1963 by fending off Rik van Looy or tugging at his jersey, depending on the version you prefer. He was drummed out of the sport within a few seasons.

Tom Simpson won in 1965 and broke a leg while skiing the next winter. That cost him not only much of the money he could have made through appearances and start money but also the wins that could keep up his value. By 1967 his place as leader in the Peugeot team was threatened and his agent, Daniel Dousset, told him he'd be commercially worthless if he didn't win or at least do well in the Tour. Simpson tried but died on Mont Ventoux.

Harm Ottenbros won in 1969 because everyone else had been more interested in stopping Eddy Merckx winning than in winning themselves. He paid for his impudence by being ostracized and he dropped out of the sport to live in a squat.

Jean-Pierre Monseré won the world championship at Leicester in 1970 and died in his rainbow jersey the following spring when he rode into a car during an unimportant race he hadn't intended to ride.

Freddy Maertens had a superb year after winning the championship in 1977 and he won again in 1981, but he won only two insignificant races between then and the end of his career in 1987.

Stephen Roche won not just the world championship in 1987 but the Tour de France and Giro as well. He then missed almost all the next season with a knee injury.

Rudy Dhaenens of Belgium won in 1990 but barely anything afterward and then retired with heart problems. He died in a car accident when he was 36.

Luc Leblanc won in 1994 and then won just one minor race in 1995.

Laurent Brochard won in 1997 and then next summer became irretrievably tangled in a doping scandal which came close to bringing the Tour de France to a halt.

Romāns Vainšteins won in 2000 and barely won a race again.

Igor Astarloa, the 2003 winner, moved to the French team, Cofidis, only for it to drop out of racing for a while when it, too, was embroiled in doping claims. He moved to other teams but without noticeable success.

Óscar Freire won in 2004 and looked like defying the curse until a saddle sore halfway through the year denied him a second consecutive title at home in Spain.

David Millar won the time trial championship in 2003 and then had it taken away the following August after it had emerged he had taken drugs in 2001 and 2003.

Isaac Gálvez was wearing the jersey he'd won as madison champion in 2006 when he hit the railing around the track at the Ghent six-day and died.

Alessandro Ballan won on the road in 2008, then fell ill and missed the spring classics and the Giro and flopped in the Tour.

But does that stop anyone wanting to win? No, sir, it doesn't! Because there's nothing to beat a rainbow jersey.

Index

Cycling's World Championships

Lightning Source UK Ltd.
Milton Keynes UK
UKOW05f1959180617

303618UK00001B/166/P

9 780985 963675